SMALL **BITES**

Publications International, Ltd.

Pictured on the front cover: Avocado Crostini *(page 124)* and Cucumber Crostini *(page 124)*.

Pictured on the back cover *(top to bottom):* Green Bean Fries *(page 76)*, Butterscotch-Chocolate Divinity *(page 180)*, Pretzel Monkey Bread *(page 108)* and Apricot and Brie Dip *(page 5)*.

ISBN: 978-1-64030-203-7

Manufactured in China.

8 7 6 5 4 3 2 1

Microwave Cooking: Microwave ovens vary in wattage. Use the cooking times as guidelines and check for doneness before adding more time.

ACKNOWLEDGMENTS
The publisher would like to thank the company listed below for the use of their recipe in this publication.

Ortega®, A Division of B&G Foods North America, Inc.

CONTENTS

CHEESY **BITES**

APRICOT AND BRIE DIP
MAKES 3 CUPS (8 TO 12 SERVINGS)

½ **cup dried apricots, finely chopped**

⅓ **cup plus 1 tablespoon apricot preserves, divided**

¼ **cup apple juice**

16 **ounces Brie cheese, rind removed and cut into cubes**

Assorted crackers

SLOW COOKER DIRECTIONS

1 Combine dried apricots, ⅓ cup preserves and apple juice in slow cooker. Cover; cook on HIGH 40 minutes.

2 Stir in cheese. Cover; cook on HIGH 30 minutes or until melted. Stir in remaining 1 tablespoon preserves. Serve with crackers.

MARINATED CHEESE

MAKES 8 SERVINGS

- **1 pound (16 ounces) feta cheese, cubed**
- **½ cup extra virgin olive oil**
- **2 tablespoons finely minced green bell pepper**
- **2 tablespoons finely minced red bell pepper**
- **2 to 3 cloves garlic, finely minced**
- **1 tablespoon chopped fresh Italian parsley**
- **2 teaspoons fresh rosemary leaves *or* 1 teaspoon dried rosemary**
- **1 teaspoon black peppercorns**
- **½ teaspoon red pepper flakes**
- **¼ teaspoon salt**
- **¼ teaspoon ground black pepper**
- **Toasted baguette slices and/or crackers**

1 Place all ingredients in clean, dry, large glass jar with tight-fitting lid. Marinate in refrigerator several hours or up to several days. Flip jar upside-down occasionally to immerse cheese in seasonings and oil.

2 Serve with toasted baguette slices, crackers, fruit or vegetables, if desired.

NOTE: As cheese is used up, additional cubed cheese can be added to jar, or remaining herb-oil mixture can be made into vinaigrette dressing by adding vinegar to the jar. Shake jar before serving.

PARMESAN-SAGE CRISPS

MAKES 8 SERVINGS

1½ cups (about 4 ounces) shredded Parmesan cheese*

2 to 3 tablespoons finely chopped fresh sage

½ teaspoon black pepper

Do not use finely grated cheese for this recipe.

1 Preheat oven to 350°F. Line baking sheets with parchment paper.

2 Combine cheese, sage and pepper in medium bowl; mix well. Place scant ⅓ cup cheese mixture on prepared baking sheet; spread into 5-inch circle. Repeat with remaining cheese mixture.

3 Bake 7 to 8 minutes or just until lightly browned. Cool on baking sheets 2 minutes or until cool enough to handle. Peel cheese crisps from paper. Cool completely. To serve, cut circles into pieces.

TIP: Serve as an appetizer or as an accompaniment to soups.

THREE-CHEESE PECAN ROLL

MAKES 2 CHEESE BALLS OR ROLLS

1 can (8 ounces) crushed pineapple in heavy syrup, drained

2 cups pecan pieces, toasted* and divided

1 package (8 ounces) cream cheese, softened

2 cups (8 ounces) finely shredded sharp Cheddar cheese

¾ cup crumbled blue cheese

2 tablespoons Worcestershire sauce (optional)

1 teaspoon sugar

½ teaspoon red pepper flakes

Assorted crackers

*To toast pecans, spread in single layer in heavy skillet. Cook over medium heat 1 to 2 minutes or until nuts are lightly browned, stirring frequently. Cool before using.

1 Combine drained pineapple, 1 cup pecans, cream cheese, Cheddar cheese, blue cheese, Worcestershire sauce, if desired, sugar and red pepper flakes in large bowl.

2 Shape mixture into 2 balls or rolls; roll in remaining pecans to coat. Wrap with plastic wrap. Freeze 30 minutes or refrigerate 2 hours or until firm. Serve with crackers.

WARM GOAT CHEESE ROUNDS

MAKES 4 SERVINGS

1 **package (4 ounces)
   goat cheese**

1 **egg**

1 **tablespoon water**

⅓ **cup seasoned dry
   bread crumbs**

1 Cut goat cheese crosswise into 8 slices. (If cheese is too difficult to slice, shape scant tablespoonfuls of cheese into balls and flatten into ¼-inch-thick rounds.)

2 Beat egg and water in small bowl. Place bread crumbs in shallow dish. Dip goat cheese rounds into egg mixture, then in bread crumbs, turning to coat all sides. Gently press bread crumbs to adhere. Place coated rounds on plate; freeze 10 minutes.

3 Cook goat cheese rounds in medium nonstick skillet over medium-high heat about 2 minutes per side or until golden brown. Serve immediately.

SERVING SUGGESTIONS: Serve goat cheese rounds with heated marinara sauce or over mixed greens tossed with vinaigrette dressing.

BAKED BRIE BITES
MAKES ABOUT 24 SERVINGS

1 **package (15 ounces) refrigerated pie crusts**

2 **tablespoons walnut chips or finely chopped walnuts**

4 **ounces Brie cheese**

2 **tablespoons honey**

½ **cup finely chopped Granny Smith apple**

1 Soften crusts according to package directions. Spray 24 mini muffin pan cups with nonstick cooking spray.

2 Preheat oven to 350°F. Unroll crusts on lightly floured surface. Cut 2-inch circles with biscuit cutter. Press dough into bottoms and up sides of prepared muffin cups.

3 Spoon ¼ teaspoon walnut chips into each crust. Cut rind off Brie; discard. Cut Brie into 24 equal pieces; roll into marble-size balls. Place 1 ball in each crust over walnut chips. Drizzle each cup with ¼ teaspoon honey.

4 Bake 12 to 15 minutes or until cheese is melted and edges are lightly browned. Cool in pan on wire rack 2 minutes. Remove from pan. Top each cup with 1 teaspoon apple. Serve immediately.

FRIED MACARONI AND CHEESE BITES

MAKES 48 PIECES (ABOUT 8 SERVINGS)

8 ounces uncooked elbow macaroni

2 tablespoons butter

2 tablespoons all-purpose flour

2 cups milk

1 teaspoon salt, divided

2 cups (8 ounces) shredded Cheddar cheese

1 cup (4 ounces) shredded Swiss cheese

1 cup (4 ounces) shredded smoked Gouda cheese

Vegetable oil for frying

3 eggs

¼ cup water

2 cups plain dry bread crumbs

1 teaspoon Italian seasoning

Marinara sauce, heated (optional)

1 Cook macaroni in large saucepan of boiling salted water 7 minutes or until al dente. Drain and set aside.

2 Melt butter in same saucepan over medium-high heat. Whisk in flour until smooth. Cook 1 minute, whisking frequently. Whisk in milk in thin steady stream; cook over medium-high heat about 8 minutes or until thickened. Add ½ teaspoon salt. Gradually stir in cheeses until melted and smooth. Stir in macaroni.

3 Spray 9-inch square baking pan with nonstick cooking spray. Spread macaroni and cheese in prepared pan. Cover with plastic wrap; refrigerate 4 hours or until firm and cold.

4 Turn out macaroni and cheese onto cutting board; cut into 48 pieces. Heat ½ inch of oil in large deep skillet or saucepan to 350°F over medium-high heat.

5 Whisk eggs and ¼ cup water in medium bowl. Combine bread crumbs, Italian seasoning and remaining ½ teaspoon salt in another medium bowl. Working with a few pieces at a time, dip macaroni and cheese pieces in egg, then toss in bread crumbs to coat. Place on large baking sheet. Dip coated pieces in egg mixture again; toss in bread crumbs to coat.

6 Fry in batches about 3 minutes or until dark brown, turning once. Remove to paper towel-lined wire rack. Return oil to 350°F between batches. Serve warm with marinara sauce for dipping, if desired.

NUTTY BACON CHEESE BALL

MAKES ABOUT 24 SERVINGS

- **1 package (8 ounces) cream cheese, softened**
- **½ cup milk**
- **2 cups (8 ounces) shredded sharp Cheddar cheese**
- **2 cups (8 ounces) shredded Monterey Jack cheese**
- **¼ cup crumbled blue cheese**
- **10 slices bacon, cooked and crumbled, divided**
- **¾ cup finely chopped pecans, divided**
- **¼ cup finely minced green onions (white parts only)**
- **1 jar (2 ounces) diced pimiento, drained**
- **Salt and black pepper**
- **¼ cup minced fresh parsley**
- **1 tablespoon poppy seeds**
- **Pita chips**

1 Beat cream cheese and milk in large bowl with electric mixer on low speed until blended. Add cheeses; beat on medium speed until well mixed. Add half of bacon, half of pecans, green onions and pimiento. Beat on medium speed until well mixed. Season with salt and pepper.

2 Transfer half of mixture to large piece of plastic wrap. Shape into a ball; wrap tightly. Repeat with remaining mixture. Refrigerate at least 2 hours or until chilled.

3 Combine remaining bacon, pecans, parsley and poppy seeds in pie plate or shallow bowl. Unwrap cheese balls; roll each in bacon mixture until well coated. Wrap balls tightly in clean plastic wrap; refrigerate up to 24 hours. Serve with pita chips.

CHIPOTLE BEER FONDUE

MAKES 8 TO 10 SERVINGS

2 cups (8 ounces) shredded Swiss cheese

2 cups (8 ounces) shredded Colby-Jack cheese

1 cup (4 ounces) shredded Gouda cheese

1 tablespoon cornstarch

1 cup Mexican beer

1 clove garlic, minced

1 to 3 canned whole chipotle peppers in adobo sauce, minced*

½ cup chopped green onions

⅛ teaspoon ground red pepper

Tortilla chips and/or French bread cubes

Cut-up vegetables

Chipotle peppers are fairly spicy so start with one and add additional peppers until you've reached your desired level of heat.

1 Toss Swiss, Colby-Jack and Gouda cheeses with cornstarch in large bowl; set aside.

2 Place beer and garlic in fondue pot or saucepan and bring to a boil over high heat. Reduce heat to low and slowly add cheese mixture, stirring constantly. Add chipotle peppers and green onions. Stir 2 to 3 minutes or until cheese is melted and mixture is smooth. Sprinkle with red pepper.

3 To serve, place fondue pot over low flame and serve with desired dippers.

GOAT CHEESE-STUFFED FIGS

MAKES 14 PIECES

7 fresh firm ripe figs*

7 slices prosciutto

**1 package (4 ounces)
    goat cheese**

Ground black pepper

*When fresh figs are not in season,
use dried figs or dates instead.
Look for dried figs in the produce
department.*

1 Preheat broiler. Line baking sheet or broiler pan with foil. Cut figs in half vertically. Cut prosciutto slices in half lengthwise to create 14 pieces (about 4 inches long and 1 inch wide).

2 Spread 1 teaspoon goat cheese onto cut side of each fig half. Wrap prosciutto slice around fig and goat cheese. Sprinkle with pepper.

3 Broil about 4 minutes or until cheese softens and figs are heated through.

CHEDDAR CRISPS

MAKES 32 CRISPS

1¾ cups all-purpose flour

½ cup yellow cornmeal

¾ teaspoon sugar

¾ teaspoon salt

½ teaspoon baking soda

½ cup (1 stick) butter

1½ cups (6 ounces) shredded sharp Cheddar cheese

½ cup cold water

2 tablespoons white vinegar

Coarsely ground black pepper

1 Combine flour, cornmeal, sugar, salt and baking soda in large bowl. Cut in butter with pastry blender or two knives until mixture resembles coarse crumbs. Stir in cheese, water and vinegar with fork until mixture forms soft dough. Cover dough; refrigerate 1 hour or freeze 30 minutes or until firm.*

2 Preheat oven to 375°F. Grease two baking sheets. Divide dough into 4 pieces. Roll each piece on floured surface into very thin 13-inch circle. Sprinkle with pepper; press pepper firmly into dough.

3 Cut each circle into 8 wedges; place on prepared baking sheets. Bake about 10 minutes or until crisp. Store in airtight container for up to 3 days.

To prepare frozen dough, thaw in the refrigerator before proceeding as directed in step 2.

BRIE BITES

MAKES 32 BITES

1 package (17¼ ounces)
   frozen puff pastry,
   thawed

¼ cup apricot preserves
   or red pepper jelly

1 round (14 ounces)
   Brie cheese (about
   5-inch diameter)

1 Preheat oven to 400°F. Cut each pastry sheet into 16 squares.

2 Spread ½ teaspoon apricot preserves on each square. Place one cube of Brie on one side of each square. Fold over opposite edge; use fork to seal edges completely. Place 1 inch apart on ungreased baking sheets.

3 Bake 10 to 13 minutes or until pastry is golden brown.

CHEESY FONDUE
MAKES 4 SERVINGS

2 cups (8 ounces) shredded Swiss cheese

2 cups (8 ounces) shredded Monterey Jack cheese

2 tablespoons all-purpose flour

1½ cups dry white wine or apple juice

Dash ground nutmeg

Dash ground red pepper

1 French bread loaf, cut into cubes

1 large Granny Smith apple, cut into wedges

1 Combine cheeses and flour in large bowl; toss lightly to coat.

2 Bring wine to a simmer over medium heat in fondue pot. Gradually add cheese mixture until melted, stirring constantly. Stir in nutmeg and red pepper. Serve with bread cubes and apple for dipping. Keep warm, stirring occasionally.

HONEY NUT BRIE

MAKES 16 TO 20 SERVINGS

¼ **cup honey**

¼ **cup coarsely chopped pecans**

1 **tablespoon brandy (optional)**

1 **round (14 ounces) Brie cheese (about 5-inch diameter)**

Water crackers and apple wedges

1 Preheat oven to 500°F. Combine honey, pecans and brandy, if desired, in small bowl. Place cheese on large round ovenproof platter or in 9-inch pie plate.

2 Bake 4 to 5 minutes or until cheese softens. Drizzle honey mixture over top of cheese. Bake 2 to 3 minutes longer or until topping is thoroughly heated. *Do not melt cheese.* Serve immediately with crackers and apples.

FRIED **FAVORITES**

TOASTED RAVIOLI
MAKES 20 TO 24 RAVIOLI

- **1 cup all-purpose flour**
- **2 eggs**
- **¼ cup water**
- **1 cup plain dry bread crumbs**
- **1 teaspoon Italian seasoning**
- **¾ teaspoon garlic powder**
- **¼ teaspoon salt**
- **½ cup grated Parmesan cheese**
- **2 tablespoons finely chopped fresh parsley**
- **Vegetable oil for frying**
- **1 package (12 to 16 ounces) meat or cheese ravioli, thawed if frozen**
- **Pasta sauce, heated**

1 Place flour in shallow bowl. Whisk eggs and water in another shallow bowl. Combine bread crumbs, Italian seasoning, garlic powder and salt in third shallow bowl. Combine cheese and parsley in large bowl; stir to blend.

2 Heat 2 inches of oil in large saucepan over medium-high heat to 350°F; adjust heat to maintain temperature.

3 Coat ravioli with flour. Dip in egg mixture, letting excess drip back into bowl. Roll in bread crumb mixture to coat.

4 Working in batches, carefully add ravioli to hot oil; cook 1 minute or until golden brown, turning once. Remove from oil with slotted spoon; drain on paper towel-lined plate. Add to bowl with cheese; toss to coat. Serve warm with sauce.

SPICY CRISPY SHRIMP

MAKES 4 SERVINGS

½ cup mayonnaise

4 teaspoons Thai chili sauce

1 teaspoon honey

½ teaspoon rice vinegar

¾ cup buttermilk

1 egg

¾ cup all-purpose flour

½ cup panko bread crumbs

1 teaspoon salt

½ teaspoon ground sage

½ teaspoon black pepper

¼ teaspoon onion powder

¼ teaspoon garlic powder

¼ teaspoon dried basil

16 to 20 large raw shrimp, peeled, deveined and patted dry

Vegetable oil for frying

2 green onions, thinly sliced (optional)

1 For sauce, combine mayonnaise, chili sauce, honey and vinegar in large bowl; mix well. Cover and refrigerate until ready to serve.

2 Whisk buttermilk and egg in medium bowl until well blended. Combine flour, panko, salt, sage, pepper, onion powder, garlic powder and basil in another medium bowl; mix well. Dip each shrimp in buttermilk mixture, then in flour mixture, turning to coat completely. Place breaded shrimp on large plate; refrigerate until oil is hot.

3 Heat 2 inches of oil in large saucepan over medium-high heat to 350°F; adjust heat to maintain temperature. Cook shrimp, 4 to 6 at a time, 2 to 3 minutes or until golden brown, turning halfway through cooking time. Drain on paper towel-lined plate.

4 Transfer shrimp to bowl with sauce; toss gently to coat. Garnish with green onions.

ONION FRITTERS WITH RAITA

MAKES 10 FRITTERS AND 1¼ CUPS SAUCE

- **8 ounces seedless cucumber (about 8 inches)**
- **1 container (7 ounces) plain 2% Greek yogurt**
- **1 clove garlic, minced**
- **2 teaspoons chopped fresh mint**
- **1 teaspoon salt, divided**
- **½ cup chickpea flour**
- **½ teaspoon baking powder**
- **¼ teaspoon cumin**
- **1 tablespoon minced fresh cilantro**
- **¼ cup water**
- **2 yellow onions, halved and thinly sliced**
- **½ cup vegetable oil**

1 For sauce, grate cucumber on large holes of box grater. Squeeze out excess water. Combine yogurt, garlic, mint and ½ teaspoon salt in medium bowl. Stir in cucumber. Refrigerate until ready to use.

2 For fritters, whisk chickpea flour, baking powder, remaining ½ teaspoon salt and cumin in large bowl. Stir in cilantro. Whisk in water in thin steady stream until batter is the consistency of heavy cream. Add additional water by teaspoons if batter is too thick. Stir in onions until coated with batter.

3 Heat oil in large cast iron skillet over medium-high heat. Working in batches, drop level ¼ cupfuls of onion mixture into hot oil. Cook about 2 minutes or until bottoms are well browned. Turn and press lightly with spatula. Cook 2 minutes or until well browned on both sides. Drain on paper towels. Serve hot with sauce.

CHEDDAR-BEER HUSH PUPPIES

MAKES ABOUT 36 HUSH PUPPIES

Vegetable oil for frying

1½ cups medium grain cornmeal

1 cup all-purpose flour

2 tablespoons sugar

1 teaspoon baking powder

1 teaspoon baking soda

1 teaspoon salt

¼ teaspoon black pepper

1 bottle (12 ounces) lager beer

1 egg, beaten

¾ cup (3 ounces) shredded Cheddar cheese

2 jalapeño peppers, seeded and minced

1 Fill large saucepan with 3 inches of oil and heat to 350°F. Line baking sheet with three layers of paper towels.

2 Whisk cornmeal, flour, sugar, baking powder, baking soda, salt and black pepper in large bowl. Whisk beer and egg in medium bowl until combined. Gradually whisk beer mixture into cornmeal mixture until smooth. Stir in cheese and jalapeños.

3 Working in batches, drop heaping tablespoonfuls of batter into oil. Fry 2 minutes or until golden brown, turning occasionally. Transfer to prepared baking sheet to drain. Repeat with remaining batter. Serve immediately.

MINI EGG ROLLS

MAKES 28 MINI EGG ROLLS

8 ounces ground pork

3 cloves garlic, minced

1 teaspoon minced
   fresh ginger

¼ teaspoon red pepper
   flakes

6 cups (12 ounces)
   shredded coleslaw
   mix

¼ cup reduced-sodium
   soy sauce

1 tablespoon cornstarch

1 tablespoon seasoned
   rice vinegar

½ cup chopped green
   onions

28 wonton wrappers

   Peanut or canola oil
   for frying

   Prepared sweet and
   sour sauce, heated

   Chinese hot mustard

1 Combine pork, garlic, ginger and red pepper flakes in large nonstick skillet; cook and stir over medium heat about 4 minutes or until pork is cooked through, stirring to break up meat. Add coleslaw mix; cover and cook 2 minutes. Uncover and cook 2 minutes or until coleslaw mix just begins to wilt.

2 Whisk soy sauce and cornstarch in small bowl until smooth and well blended; stir into pork mixture. Add vinegar; cook 2 to 3 minutes or until sauce is thickened. Remove from heat; stir in green onions.

3 Working with one wonton wrapper at a time, place wrapper on clean work surface. Spoon 1 level tablespoon pork mixture across and just below center of wrapper. Fold bottom point of wrapper up over filling; fold side points over filling, forming envelope shape. Moisten inside edges of top point with water and roll egg roll toward top point, pressing firmly to seal. Repeat with remaining wrappers and filling.

4 Pour oil into large skillet to depth of ¼ inch; heat over medium heat. Fry egg rolls in small batches 2 minutes per side or until golden brown. Remove with slotted spoon and drain on paper towels. Serve immediately with sweet and sour sauce and mustard for dipping.

CORN FRITTERS WITH TOMATO SAUCE

MAKES 4 SERVINGS

1 tablespoon vegetable oil

1 small red onion, very thinly sliced

1 cup grape tomatoes, halved or 1 cup canned diced tomatoes, drained

2 teaspoons balsamic or cider vinegar

1 tablespoon capers

¾ teaspoon salt, divided

1¼ teaspoons sugar, divided

⅛ teaspoon black pepper

½ cup all-purpose flour

½ teaspoon baking powder

⅛ teaspoon dried thyme

Pinch ground red pepper (optional)

1 egg

¼ cup half-and-half or milk

1 cup cooked corn kernels from 1 large ear or 1 cup frozen corn, thawed

Vegetable oil for frying

1 For sauce, heat 1 tablespoon oil in large nonstick skillet. Add onion; cook and stir over medium-high heat 3 to 5 minutes or until tender. Add tomatoes. Cook 2 to 3 minutes or until very soft. Remove from heat. Stir in vinegar, capers, ¼ teaspoon sugar, ¼ teaspoon salt and black pepper. Keep warm.

2 Mix flour, remaining 1 teaspoon sugar, baking powder, remaining ½ teaspoon salt, thyme and red pepper, if desired, in large bowl. Beat egg and half-and-half in small bowl. Add to flour mixture. Stir to mix. Don't beat. Stir in corn.

3 Pour oil ¼-inch deep in large skillet. Heat over medium heat until drop of batter sizzles and turns golden in less than a minute. Drop batter by rounded tablespoons into hot oil. Fry on first side 3 minutes or until golden. Turn. Fry on second side 1 minute more or until golden.

4 Remove fritters with slotted spoon. Drain on platter lined with paper towels. Serve hot with tomato sauce on the side.

ARANCINI
MAKES 4 SERVINGS

4 cups chicken or vegetable broth

2 tablespoons butter

2 tablespoons olive oil

1 shallot, minced

1 cup uncooked arborio rice

¼ cup dry white wine

1 generous pinch saffron threads, ground to a powder

¼ cup grated Parmesan cheese

Salt and black pepper

1½ cups Italian seasoned dry bread crumbs

3 egg whites

12 (½-inch) pieces fresh mozzarella cheese

12 (½-inch) pieces Parmigiano-Reggiano cheese

12 (¼-inch) cubes ham

2 cups canola oil

1 Bring broth to a simmer in medium saucepan over medium heat; keep warm.

2 Heat butter and oil in large saucepan over medium-high heat. Add shallot; cook and stir 30 seconds or just until beginning to brown. Add rice; cook and stir 1 to 2 minutes or until edges of rice become translucent. Add wine and saffron; cook and stir until wine evaporates.

3 Reduce heat to medium-low. Add ½ cup broth, stirring constantly until broth is absorbed. Repeat until all broth is used. Stir in Parmesan cheese. Season with salt and pepper. Spread on large baking sheet; cool completely.

4 Spread bread crumbs on plate. Beat egg whites in small bowl.

5 Line baking sheet with waxed paper. Working with 2 tablespoons risotto at a time, flatten into 3-inch disc. Place one piece of each cheese and ham in center of disc. Fold edges up to cover filling, gently pinching seams to seal. Roll between palms to form oval.

6 Roll in bread crumbs, then dip in egg whites to coat. Roll again in bread crumbs. Place on prepared baking sheet. Repeat with remaining ingredients. Cover and refrigerate 1 hour or overnight.

7 Heat oil in large deep skillet to 360°F. Cook arancini 1 minute per side or until golden brown. Transfer to wire rack. Serve warm.

MINI CRAB AND CREAM CHEESE FLAUTAS

MAKES 24 MINI FLAUTAS

2 cups vegetable oil

1 package (8 ounces) pasteurized crabmeat, drained

1 can (4 ounces) ORTEGA® Fired-Roasted Diced Green Chiles, drained

4 ounces cream cheese, softened

6 (8-inch) ORTEGA® Flour Soft Tortillas

1 cup sour cream

½ cup ORTEGA® Salsa Verde

HEAT oil in medium saucepan over medium-high heat to 375°F. Line platter with paper towels.

COMBINE crabmeat, chiles and cream cheese in medium bowl.

SPREAD about ¼ cup mixture down middle of tortilla and firmly roll like a cigar. Keep tortilla roll closed with 4 toothpicks. Cut between toothpicks into four equal pieces; set aside. Repeat with remaining filling and tortillas.

PLACE pieces carefully into hot oil. Cook 1 minute or until golden brown, turning once. Remove with slotted spoon. Drain on paper towels.

COMBINE sour cream and salsa verde in small bowl; mix well. Serve with flautas as dip.

TIP: Serve some ORTEGA® Guacamole Style Dip too, and encourage double dipping!

CRAB CAKES

MAKES 12 CAKES

CRAB CAKES

1 package (3 ounces) shrimp-flavored ramen noodles

1 egg

¼ cup mayonnaise

1 tablespoon chopped fresh dill

2 teaspoons fresh lemon juice

1 pound fresh crabmeat, drained and picked

2 tablespoons butter

2 tablespoons olive oil

LEMON DILL DIPPING SAUCE

½ cup plain Greek yogurt

Juice of 1 lemon

1 tablespoon olive oil

1 tablespoon chopped fresh dill

½ teaspoon salt

1 For crab cakes, place ramen noodles in food processor; process until crumbs form. Place crumbs in large bowl; add ramen seasoning packet, egg, mayonnaise, 1 tablespoon dill and 2 teaspoons lemon juice; stir well. Fold in crabmeat; refrigerate 1 hour.

2 Shape mixture into 12 patties. Heat 1 tablespoon butter and 1 tablespoon oil in large nonstick skillet over medium-high heat. Cook half of patties 5 minutes per side or until golden brown. Repeat with remaining butter, oil and patties.

3 For sauce, combine yogurt, juice of 1 lemon, oil, 1 tablespoon dill and salt in small bowl; stir well. Serve with crab cakes.

CLASSIC HUSH PUPPIES

MAKES ABOUT 24 HUSH PUPPIES

1½ cups yellow cornmeal

½ cup all-purpose flour

2 teaspoons baking powder

¾ teaspoon salt

1 cup milk

1 small onion, minced

1 egg, lightly beaten

Vegetable oil for frying

1 Combine cornmeal, flour, baking powder and salt in medium bowl; mix well. Add milk, onion and egg; stir until well blended. Let batter stand 5 to 10 minutes.

2 Heat 1 inch of oil in large heavy skillet over medium heat to 375°F; adjust heat to maintain temperature. Drop batter by tablespoonfuls into hot oil. Cook in batches 2 minutes or until golden brown. Drain on paper towel-lined plate. Serve warm.

CAPER-RICE CROQUETTES

MAKES 6 SERVINGS

⅔ cup water

⅓ cup uncooked white
   rice

2 ounces prosciutto
   slices, finely
   chopped

1 egg yolk, beaten

1 tablespoons capers,
   drained and rinsed

⅛ teaspoon salt

⅛ teaspoon dried
   oregano

⅛ teaspoon black
   pepper

⅔ cup fresh bread
   crumbs

1 tablespoon butter

1 tablespoon olive oil

1 Bring water to a boil in small saucepan over high heat. Stir in rice. Reduce heat to low; cover and simmer about 14 minutes or until rice is tender and water is absorbed. Transfer rice to medium bowl; cool until almost room temperature.

2 Add prosciutto, egg yolk, capers, salt, oregano and pepper; mix well. Spread bread crumbs on large plate. Shape rice mixture into 18 balls 1¼ inches in diameter. Flatten slightly; carefully coat with bread crumbs. Place on plate; refrigerate 15 to 30 minutes until firm.

3 Heat butter and oil in heavy medium skillet over medium-high heat until butter melts. Add half of croquettes; cook 2 to 3 minutes or until golden brown. Turn and cook 1 to 2 minutes or until golden brown. Remove to plate; keep warm. Repeat with remaining croquettes, adding additional butter if necessary. Serve hot.

MANCHEGO CHEESE CROQUETTES

MAKES 6 SERVINGS

¼ cup (½ stick) butter

1 tablespoon minced shallot or onion

½ cup all-purpose flour

¾ cup milk

½ cup grated manchego cheese or Parmesan cheese, divided

¼ teaspoon salt

¼ teaspoon smoked or regular paprika

⅛ teaspoon ground nutmeg

1 egg

½ cup plain dry bread crumbs

Vegetable oil for frying

1 Melt butter in medium skillet over medium heat. Add shallot; cook and stir 2 minutes. Stir in flour; cook and stir 2 minutes. Gradually whisk in milk; cook until mixture comes to a boil, whisking frequently. Remove from heat. Stir in ¼ cup cheese, salt, paprika and nutmeg. Transfer mixture to small bowl; cover and refrigerate several hours or up to 24 hours.

2 Shape teaspoonfuls of dough into 1-inch balls with lightly floured hands.

3 Beat egg in shallow bowl. Combine bread crumbs and remaining ¼ cup cheese in second shallow bowl. Dip each ball into egg, then roll in bread crumb mixture.

4 Heat ¼ cup oil in medium skillet over medium-high heat. Cook croquettes in batches until brown on all sides, replenishing oil as needed. Drain on paper towels. Serve warm.

NOTE: Cooked croquettes may be kept warm in a 200°F oven up to 30 minutes before serving.

CURLY CURRY CHIPS

MAKES 4 SERVINGS

- **4 small or 2 large russet potatoes, peeled**
- **1 teaspoon vegetable oil**
- **¾ teaspoon salt, divided**
- **1 tablespoon butter**
- **¼ cup finely chopped onion**
- **1 tablespoon all-purpose flour**
- **1 tablespoon curry powder**
- **1 cup vegetable broth**

1 Preheat oven to 450°F. Line large baking sheet with parchment paper. Spiral potatoes with thick spiral blade of spiralizer.* Spread potatoes on prepared baking sheet; drizzle with oil. Bake about 30 minutes or until golden brown and crispy, turning once. Sprinkle with ½ teaspoon salt.

2 Melt butter in small saucepan over medium-high heat. Add onion; cook and stir about 3 minutes or until softened. Whisk in flour and curry powder until well blended; cook 1 minute, stirring constantly. Add broth in thin steady stream, whisking constantly.

3 Reduce heat to medium; cook about 10 minutes or until thick. Taste and add ¼ teaspoon salt, if desired. For smoother sauce, cool slightly and purée in blender or food processor. Serve with potatoes.

*If you don't have a spiralizer, make regular oven fries instead. Peel potatoes and cut lengthwise into ¼-inch strips. Place in colander; rinse under cold water 2 minutes. Pay dry with paper towels. Place on prepared baking sheet. Drizzle with 2 teaspoons vegetable oil and toss to coat. Spread in single layer on baking sheet. Bake about 25 minutes or until golden crown and crispy, turning once.

GARLIC BITES

MAKES ABOUT 24 BITES

½ of 16-ounce package frozen phyllo dough, thawed to room temperature

¾ cup (1½ sticks) butter, melted

3 large heads garlic, separated into cloves and peeled

½ cup finely chopped walnuts

1 cup Italian-style bread crumbs

1 Preheat oven to 350°F. Remove phyllo from package; unroll and place on large sheet of waxed paper. Cut phyllo crosswise into 2-inch-wide strips. Cover phyllo with large sheet of plastic wrap and damp, clean kitchen towel. (Phyllo dries out quickly if not covered.)

2 Lay 1 strip of phyllo at a time on flat surface and brush immediately with melted butter. Place 1 clove of garlic at end. Sprinkle 1 teaspoon walnuts along length of strip.

3 Roll up garlic clove and walnuts in strip, tucking in side edges as you roll. Brush with butter; roll in bread crumbs. Repeat with remaining phyllo, garlic, walnuts and butter.

4 Place on rack in shallow roasting pan. Bake 20 minutes. Serve warm.

CRUNCHY PARMESAN ZUCCHINI STICKS

MAKES 24 STICKS

3 medium zucchini

1 package (3 ounces) ramen noodles, any flavor

½ cup shredded Parmesan cheese

½ cup all-purpose flour

1 egg

1 tablespoon water

Marinara sauce, warmed

1 Preheat oven to 400°F. Line baking sheet with parchment paper. Cut zucchini in half crosswise, then cut each half into 4 sticks.

2 Place noodles and cheese in food processor; pulse until fine crumbs form. Place in shallow bowl.

3 Combine flour and ramen seasoning packet in another shallow bowl. Whisk egg and water in third shallow bowl.

4 Coat zucchini sticks with flour mixture. Dip in egg mixture, letting excess drip back into bowl. Roll in ramen mixture to coat.

5 Bake 20 minutes or until zucchini is soft and coating is golden brown. Serve warm with marinara sauce for dipping.

GUACAMOLE BITES

MAKES 24 BITES

2 tablespoons vegetable oil

1¼ teaspoons salt, divided

½ teaspoon garlic powder

12 (6-inch) corn tortillas

2 small ripe avocados

2 tablespoons finely chopped onion

1 tablespoon chopped fresh cilantro

2 teaspoons lime juice

1 teaspoon finely chopped jalapeño pepper *or* ¼ teaspoon hot pepper sauce

1 Preheat oven to 375°F. Whisk oil, ¾ teaspoon salt and garlic powder in small bowl until well blended.

2 Use 3-inch biscuit cutter to cut out 2 circles from each tortilla to create 24 circles total. Wrap stack of tortilla circles loosely in waxed paper; microwave on HIGH 10 to 15 seconds or just until softened. Brush one side of each tortilla very lightly with oil mixture; press into 24 mini (1¾-inch) muffin cups, oiled side up. (Do not spray muffin cups with nonstick cooking spray.)

3 Bake about 8 minutes or until crisp. Remove to wire racks to cool.

4 Meanwhile, prepare guacamole. Cut avocados in half; remove pits. Scoop pulp into large bowl; mash roughly, leaving slightly chunky. Stir in onion, cilantro, lime juice, remaining ½ teaspoon salt and jalapeño.

5 Fill each tortilla cup with 2 to 3 teaspoons guacamole.

MOZZARELLA STICKS

MAKES 12 STICKS

¼ cup all-purpose flour

2 eggs

1 tablespoon water

1 cup plain dry bread crumbs

2 teaspoons Italian seasoning

½ teaspoon salt

½ teaspoon garlic powder

1 package (12 ounces) string cheese (12 sticks)

Vegetable oil for frying

1 cup marinara or pizza sauce, heated

1 Place flour in shallow bowl. Whisk eggs and water in another shallow bowl. Combine bread crumbs, Italian seasoning, salt and garlic powder in third shallow bowl.

2 Coat each piece of cheese with flour. Dip in egg mixture, letting excess drip back into bowl. Roll in bread crumb mixture to coat. Dip again in egg mixture and roll again in bread crumb mixture. Refrigerate until ready to cook.

3 Line wire rack with paper towels. Heat 2 inches of oil in large saucepan over medium-high heat to 350°F; adjust heat to maintain temperature. Add cheese sticks; cook about 1 minute or until golden brown. Drain on wire rack. Serve with warm sauce for dipping.

LITTLE RIBS IN PAPRIKA SAUCE

MAKES 6 TO 8 SERVINGS

1 rack pork baby back ribs (about 1½ pounds), cut into individual pieces

1 can (about 14 ounces) chicken broth

1 cup dry white wine or beer

1 tablespoon olive oil

2 teaspoons dried oregano

2 teaspoons smoked or regular paprika

4 cloves garlic, minced

½ teaspoon salt

¼ teaspoon black pepper

1 Place ribs, broth, wine, oil, oregano, paprika, garlic, salt and pepper in large saucepan. Bring to a boil over medium-high heat. Reduce heat to low. Simmer, covered, 1 hour or until meat is tender and begins to separate from bones.

2 Remove ribs to serving plate; keep warm. Skim and discard fat from cooking liquid. Bring to a boil over medium heat. Reduce heat to low; simmer until sauce is reduced by half. Spoon sauce over ribs.

POTATO SKINS

MAKES 16 PIECES

- **8 medium baking potatoes (6 to 8 ounces each)**
- **1 tablespoon vegetable oil**
- **1 teaspoon salt**
- **⅛ teaspoon black pepper**
- **1 tablespoon butter, melted**
- **1 cup (4 ounces) shredded Cheddar cheese**
- **8 slices bacon, crisp-cooked and coarsely chopped**
- **1 cup sour cream**
- **3 tablespoons snipped fresh chives**

1 Preheat oven to 400°F.

2 Prick potatoes all over with fork. Rub oil over potatoes; sprinkle with salt and pepper. Place in 13×9-inch baking pan. Bake 1 hour or until fork-tender. Let stand until cool enough to handle. *Reduce oven temperature to 350°F.*

3 Cut potatoes in half lengthwise; cut small slice off bottom of each half so potato halves will lay flat. Scoop out soft middles of potato skins; reserve for another use. Place potato halves skin sides up in baking pan; brush potato skins with butter.

4 Bake 20 to 25 minutes or until crisp. Turn potatoes over; top with cheese and bacon. Bake 5 minutes or until cheese is melted. Cool slightly. Top with sour cream and chives just before serving.

DUO OF MINI CHEESEBURGERS

MAKES 4 SERVINGS

8 ounces ground turkey

1 teaspoon chili powder

8 ounces ground beef

2 tablespoons minced onion

¼ teaspoon black pepper

2 tablespoons salsa

1 tablespoon hickory-flavored barbecue sauce

4 slices Cheddar or American cheese, halved diagonally

8 small whole wheat dinner rolls, split and lightly toasted

1 Preheat broiler. Line baking sheet with foil.

2 Combine turkey and chili powder in medium bowl; mix well. Shape into 4 patties about 3 inches in diameter and ½ inch thick. Place on prepared baking sheet.

3 Combine beef, onion and pepper in separate medium bowl; mix well. Shape into 4 patties. Place on baking sheet with turkey patties.

4 Broil patties 4 minutes per side or until no longer pink in center. Spoon salsa over turkey patties and barbecue sauce over beef patties; top all with cheese. Broil 1 minute or until cheese is melted. Serve in rolls.

BUFFALO WINGS

MAKES 4 SERVINGS

1 cup hot pepper sauce

⅓ cup vegetable oil, plus additional for frying

1 teaspoon sugar

½ teaspoon ground red pepper

½ teaspoon garlic powder

½ teaspoon Worcestershire sauce

⅛ teaspoon black pepper

1 pound chicken wings, tips discarded, separated at joints

Blue cheese or ranch dressing

Celery sticks

1 Combine hot pepper sauce, ⅓ cup oil, sugar, red pepper, garlic powder, Worcestershire sauce and black pepper in small saucepan; cook over medium heat 20 minutes. Remove from heat; pour sauce into large bowl.

2 Heat 3 inches of oil in large saucepan over medium-high heat to 350°F; adjust heat to maintain temperature. Add wings; cook 10 minutes or until crispy. Drain on wire rack set over paper towels.

3 Transfer wings to bowl of sauce; toss to coat. Serve with blue cheese dressing and celery sticks.

CHICKEN BACON QUESADILLAS

MAKES 4 SERVINGS

4 teaspoons vegetable oil, divided

4 (8-inch) flour tortillas

1 cup (4 ounces) shredded Colby-Jack cheese

2 cups coarsely chopped cooked chicken

4 slices bacon, crisp-cooked and coarsely chopped

½ cup pico de gallo, plus additional for serving

Sour cream and guacamole

1 Heat large nonstick skillet over medium heat; brush with 1 teaspoon oil. Place one tortilla in skillet; sprinkle with ¼ cup cheese. Spread ½ cup chicken over one half of tortilla; top with one fourth of bacon and 2 tablespoons pico de gallo.

2 Cook 1 to 2 minutes or until cheese is melted and bottom of tortilla is lightly browned. Fold tortilla over filling, pressing with spatula. Transfer to cutting board; cool slightly. Cut into wedges. Repeat with remaining ingredients. Serve with additional pico de gallo, sour cream and guacamole.

GREEN BEAN FRIES

MAKES 4 TO 6 SERVINGS

CUCUMBER RANCH DIP

½ cup mayonnaise

¼ cup sour cream

¼ cup buttermilk

¼ cup minced peeled cucumber

1½ teaspoons lemon juice

1 clove garlic

½ teaspoon dried dill weed

½ teaspoon dried parsley flakes

½ teaspoon salt

⅛ teaspoon ground red pepper

GREEN BEAN FRIES

8 ounces fresh green beans, trimmed

½ cup all-purpose flour

½ cup cornstarch

¾ cup milk

1 egg

1 cup plain dry bread crumbs

1 teaspoon salt

½ teaspoon onion powder

¼ teaspoon garlic powder

Vegetable oil for frying

1 For dip, combine mayonnaise, sour cream, buttermilk, cucumber, lemon juice, garlic, dill, parsley flakes, salt and red pepper in blender; blend until smooth. Refrigerate until ready to use.

2 Bring large saucepan of salted water to a boil. Add green beans; cook 4 minutes or until crisp-tender. Drain and rinse under cold water to stop cooking.

3 Combine flour and cornstarch in large bowl. Whisk milk and egg in another large bowl. Combine bread crumbs, salt, onion powder and garlic powder in shallow bowl. Place green beans in flour mixture; toss to coat. Working in batches, coat beans with egg mixture, letting excess drain back into bowl. Roll beans in bread crumb mixture to coat. Place on large baking sheet.

4 Heat 3 inches of oil in large saucepan over medium-high heat to 375°F. Cook green beans in batches about 1 minute or until golden brown; adjust heat to maintain temperature. Drain on paper towel-lined wire rack. Serve with dip.

TIP: To save time, you can substitute prepared ranch dressing for the homemade dip.

PRETZEL STICKS WITH BEER-CHEESE DIP

MAKES 6 TO 8 SERVINGS (2 CUPS DIP)

PRETZELS

1⅔ cups warm water (110° to 115°F)

1 package (¼ ounce) active dry yeast

2 teaspoons sugar

1 teaspoon table salt

4½ cups all-purpose flour, plus additional for work surface

2 tablespoons butter, softened

2 tablespoons vegetable oil

12 cups water

½ cup baking soda

Kosher salt or pretzel salt and sesame seeds

HONEY–MUSTARD DIP

⅓ cup sour cream

¼ cup Dijon mustard

3 tablespoons honey

BEER–CHEESE DIP

2 tablespoons butter

1 clove garlic, minced

2 tablespoons all-purpose flour

1 tablespoon Dijon mustard

1 teaspoon Worcestershire sauce

1 cup Belgian white ale

2 cups (8 ounces) shredded white Cheddar cheese

1 cup (4 ounces) shredded Monterey Jack cheese

Black pepper (optional)

1 Combine 1⅔ cups warm water, yeast, sugar and table salt in large bowl; mix well. Let stand 5 minutes or until bubbly. Add 4½ cups flour and butter; beat with electric mixer on low speed until combined, scraping side of bowl occasionally. Replace paddle attachment with dough hook; knead on medium-low speed 5 minutes.

2 Place dough in large greased bowl; turn to grease top. Cover and let rise in warm place 1 hour or until doubled in size.

3 For honey-mustard dip, combine sour cream, ¼ cup mustard and honey in small bowl; mix well. Refrigerate until ready to use.

4 Preheat oven to 450°F. Brush 1 tablespoon oil over each of two large baking sheets. Bring 12 cups water to a boil in large saucepan or Dutch oven.

5 Punch down dough; turn out onto floured work surface. Divide dough into 14 equal pieces. Roll each piece into 12-inch-long rope. Cut each rope in half.

6 Carefully stir baking soda into boiling water. Working in batches, drop dough pieces into boiling water; cook 30 seconds. Remove to prepared baking sheets with slotted spoon. Make 3 to 4 slashes in each pretzel stick with sharp knife. Sprinkle with kosher salt and sesame seeds. Bake 14 to 15 minutes or until dark golden brown, rotating baking sheets halfway through baking time. Cool slightly on wire rack.

7 Meanwhile for beer-cheese dip, melt 2 tablespoons butter in medium saucepan over medium heat. Add garlic; cook and stir 1 minute. Whisk in 2 tablespoons flour until well blended; cook 1 minute. Whisk in 1 tablespoon mustard and Worcestershire sauce. Gradually whisk in ale in thin steady stream. Cook 1 minute or until slightly thickened. Add cheeses by ¼ cupfuls, stirring until cheeses are melted after each addition. Transfer to serving bowl; sprinkle with pepper, if desired. Serve pretzels with dips.

ONION RING STACK
MAKES ABOUT 20 ONION RINGS

1 cup all-purpose flour, divided

½ cup cornmeal

1 teaspoon black pepper

½ teaspoon salt

¼ to ½ teaspoon ground red pepper

1 cup light-colored beer

Rémoulade sauce (recipe follows) and/or ranch dressing

Vegetable oil for frying

¼ cup plus 2 tablespoons cornstarch, divided

2 large sweet onions, cut into ½-inch rings and separated

1 Combine ½ cup flour, cornmeal, black pepper, salt and red pepper in large bowl; mix well. Whisk in beer until well blended. Let stand 1 hour. Prepare rémoulade sauce.

2 Heat 2 inches of oil in large saucepan over medium-high heat to 360°F to 370°F. Line large wire rack with paper towels.

3 Whisk ¼ cup cornstarch into batter. Combine remaining ½ cup flour and 2 tablespoons cornstarch in medium bowl. Thoroughly coat onions with flour mixture.

4 Working with one at a time, dip onion rings into batter to coat completely and carefully place in hot oil. Cook about 4 onions rings at a time 3 minutes or until golden brown, turning once. Remove to prepared wire rack; season with additional salt. Return oil to 370°F between batches. Serve with rémoulade sauce.

RÉMOULADE SAUCE: Combine 1 cup mayonnaise, 2 tablespoons coarse-grain mustard, 1 tablespoon lemon juice, 1 tablespoon sweet relish, 1 teaspoon Worcestershire sauce, 1 teaspoon horseradish sauce and ¼ teaspoon hot pepper sauce in medium bowl; mix well.

CARAMELIZED BACON

MAKES 6 SERVINGS

---

12 slices (about 12 ounces) applewood-smoked bacon

½ cup packed brown sugar

2 tablespoons water

¼ to ½ teaspoon ground red pepper

1 Preheat oven to 375°F. Line 15×10-inch baking sheet with heavy-duty foil. Spray wire rack with nonstick cooking spray; place on baking sheet.

2 Cut bacon in half crosswise, if desired; arrange in single layer on prepared wire rack. Combine brown sugar, water and red pepper in small bowl; mix well. Brush generously over bacon.

3 Bake 20 to 25 minutes or until bacon is well browned. Immediately remove to serving platter; cool completely.

NOTE: Bacon can be prepared up to 3 days ahead and stored in the refrigerator between sheets of waxed paper in a resealable food storage bag. Let stand at room temperature at least 30 minutes before serving.

BREAD **BITES**

MAPLE BACON MONKEY BREAD
MAKES 12 SERVINGS

10 slices bacon, crisp-cooked and coarsely chopped (about 12 ounces)

⅓ cup packed brown sugar

¼ teaspoon black pepper

3 tablespoons butter

3 tablespoons maple syrup

1 loaf (1 pound) frozen bread dough, thawed according to package directions

1 Spray 12-cup (10-inch) bundt pan with nonstick cooking spray.

2 Combine bacon, brown sugar and pepper in medium bowl. Combine butter and maple syrup in medium microwavable bowl; microwave on HIGH 30 seconds; stir. Microwave 20 seconds or until butter is melted.

3 Roll dough into 1-inch balls. Dip balls in butter mixture; roll in bacon mixture to coat. Layer in prepared pan. Reheat any remaining butter mixture, if necessary; drizzle over top of dough. Cover and let rise in warm place about 45 minutes or until doubled in size. Preheat oven to 350°F.

4 Bake 30 to 35 minutes or until golden brown. Cool in pan on wire rack 5 minutes. Loosen edges of bread with knife; invert onto serving plate. Serve warm.

CHEESY GARLIC BREAD

MAKES 8 TO 10 SERVINGS

1 loaf (about 16 ounces) Italian bread

½ cup (1 stick) butter, softened

8 cloves garlic, very thinly sliced

¼ cup grated Parmesan cheese

2 cups (8 ounces) shredded mozzarella cheese

1 Preheat oven to 425°F. Line large baking sheet with foil.

2 Cut bread in half horizontally. Spread cut sides of bread evenly with butter; top with sliced garlic. Sprinkle with Parmesan, then mozzarella. Place on prepared baking sheet.

3 Bake about 12 minutes or until cheeses are melted and golden brown in spots. Cut crosswise into slices. Serve warm.

MINI PIZZAS

MAKES 20 PIZZAS

1 package (12 ounces) refrigerated flaky buttermilk biscuits (10 biscuits)

80 mini pepperoni slices or 20 small pepperoni slices

8 to 10 pickled jalapeño pepper slices, chopped (optional)

1 tablespoon dried basil

½ cup pizza sauce

1½ cups (6 ounces) shredded mozzarella cheese

Shredded Parmesan cheese (optional)

1 Preheat oven to 400°F. Spray 20 standard (2½-inch) nonstick muffin cups with nonstick cooking spray.

2 Separate biscuits; split each biscuit in half horizontally to create 20 rounds. Place in prepared muffin cups. Press 4 mini pepperoni slices into center of each round. Sprinkle with jalapeños, if desired, and basil. Spread pizza sauce over pepperoni; sprinkle with mozzarella.

3 Bake 8 to 9 minutes or until bottoms of pizzas are golden brown. Sprinkle with Parmesan, if desired. Cool in pan 2 minutes; remove to wire racks. Serve warm.

ANTIPASTO BISCUIT STICKS
MAKES 8 BISCUIT STICKS

- **2 cups biscuit baking mix**
- **½ teaspoon dried oregano**
- **2 tablespoons cold butter, cut into thin slices**
- **½ to ⅔ cup milk**
- **¼ cup finely chopped pimiento-stuffed olives**
- **¼ cup finely chopped salami***
- **¼ cup finely chopped or shredded provolone cheese**

*Hard salami is too chewy for these biscuits; use sandwich salami.

1 Preheat oven to 425°F. Line baking sheet with parchment paper or spray with nonstick cooking spray; set aside.

2 Combine biscuit mix and oregano in large bowl. Cut in butter with pastry blender or two knives until mixture resembles coarse crumbs. Gradually stir in enough milk to form slightly sticky dough. Gently knead in olives, salami and cheese.

3 Turn dough out onto very lightly floured surface; pat into rectangle about ¾ inch thick. Cut dough into 8 strips with sharp knife; gently roll each strip into rounded breadstick shape. Place 1 inch apart on prepared baking sheet.

4 Bake 11 to 14 minutes or until golden brown. Remove to wire rack to cool.

VARIATION: For regular biscuits, cut dough with 2½-inch biscuit cutter, reworking dough as necessary to make 8 biscuits. Proceed as directed above.

SERVING SUGGESTION: For a delicious appetizer, serve the biscuit sticks with marinara sauce or extra virgin olive oil for dipping.

BUTTERMILK DROP BISCUITS

MAKES 9 BISCUITS

2 cups all-purpose flour

2 teaspoons baking powder

1 teaspoon sugar

½ teaspoon salt

¼ teaspoon baking soda

1 cup buttermilk

5 tablespoons unsalted butter, melted, divided

1 Preheat oven to 450°F. Spray baking sheet with nonstick cooking spray.

2 Combine flour, baking powder, sugar, salt and baking soda in large bowl; mix well. Whisk buttermilk and 4 tablespoons butter in small bowl until well blended. Stir into flour mixture until combined.

3 Using ¼ cup measuring cup sprayed with nonstick cooking spray, drop biscuits 1½ inches apart onto prepared baking sheet.

4 Bake 12 minutes or until tops are golden brown. Brush tops with remaining 1 tablespoon butter. Cool on baking sheets 5 minutes; serve warm or cool completely.

PULL-APART GARLIC CHEESE BREAD

MAKES 12 SERVINGS

- **3 cups all-purpose flour**
- **1 package (¼ ounce) rapid-rise active dry yeast**
- **1 teaspoon salt**
- **1 cup warm water (120°F)**
- **2 tablespoons olive oil**
- **6 cloves garlic, minced, divided**
- **¼ cup (½ stick) butter**
- **¼ teaspoon paprika**
- **1 cup grated Parmesan cheese**
- **1 cup (4 ounces) shredded mozzarella cheese**
- **½ cup pizza sauce**
- **Chopped fresh parsley (optional)**

1. Combine flour, yeast and salt in large bowl of electric stand mixer. Stir in water and oil to form rough dough; add half of garlic. Knead with dough hook on low speed 5 to 7 minutes or until dough is smooth and elastic.

2. Shape dough into a ball. Place in large greased bowl; turn to grease top. Cover and let rise in warm place 45 minutes or until doubled in size.

3. Melt butter in small skillet over medium-low heat. Add remaining garlic; cook and stir 1 minute. Stir in paprika; remove from heat. Brush 9-inch springform pan with some of butter mixture. Place 6-ounce ramekin in center of pan. Line baking sheet with foil. Place Parmesan in shallow bowl.

4. Turn out dough onto lightly floured surface; pat into 9-inch square. Cut into 1-inch squares; roll into balls. Dip half of balls in melted butter mixture; roll in Parmesan to coat. Place around ramekin in prepared pan; sprinkle with ½ cup mozzarella. Repeat with remaining dough and mozzarella. Cover and let rise in warm place 1 hour or until dough has risen to top of pan. Preheat oven to 350°F. Pour pizza sauce into ramekin. Place springform pan on prepared baking sheet.

5. Bake 20 to 25 minutes or until bread is firm and golden brown. Loosen edges of bread with knife; carefully remove side of pan. Sprinkle with parsley, if desired. Serve warm.

SPINACH ARTICHOKE FLATBREAD

MAKES 8 SERVINGS

- **1 tablespoon olive oil**
- **2 cloves garlic, minced**
- **1 package (10 ounces) baby spinach**
- **1 can (about 14 ounces) artichoke quarters, drained and sliced**
- **½ teaspoon salt**
- **¼ teaspoon dried oregano**
- **Black pepper**
- **Red pepper flakes**
- **2 rectangular pizza or flatbread crusts (about 8 ounces each)**
- **1 plum tomato, seeded and diced**
- **2 cups (8 ounces) shredded Monterey Jack cheese**
- **½ cup (2 ounces) shredded Italian cheese blend**
- **Shredded fresh basil (optional)**

1 Preheat oven to 425°F.

2 Heat oil in large nonstick skillet over medium-high heat. Add garlic; cook and stir 30 seconds. Add half of spinach; cook and stir until slightly wilted. Add additional spinach by handfuls; cook about 3 minutes or until completely wilted, stirring occasionally. Transfer to medium bowl; stir in artichokes, salt and oregano. Season with black pepper and red pepper flakes.

3 Place pizza crusts on large baking sheet. Spread spinach mixture over crusts; sprinkle evenly with tomatoes, Monterey Jack cheese and Italian cheese blend.

4 Bake 12 minutes or until cheese is melted and edges are browned. Garnish with basil.

TIP: For crispier crust, bake flatbreads on a preheated pizza stone or directly on the oven rack.

GARLIC KNOTS

MAKES 20 KNOTS

- ¾ **cup warm water (105° to 115°F)**
- 1 **package (¼ ounce) active dry yeast**
- 1 **teaspoon sugar**
- 2¼ **cups all-purpose flour**
- 2 **tablespoons olive oil, divided**
- 1½ **teaspoons salt, divided**
- 4 **tablespoons (½ stick) butter, divided**
- 1 **tablespoon minced garlic**
- ¼ **teaspoon garlic powder**
- ½ **cup grated Parmesan cheese**
- 2 **tablespoons chopped fresh parsley**
- ½ **teaspoon dried oregano**

1 Combine water, yeast and sugar in large bowl of electric stand mixer; stir to dissolve yeast. Let stand 5 minutes or until bubbly. Stir in flour, 1 tablespoon oil and 1 teaspoon salt; knead with dough hook at low speed 5 minutes or until dough is smooth and elastic. Shape dough into a ball. Place in large lightly greased bowl; turn to grease top. Cover and let rise 1 hour or until doubled in size.

2 Melt 2 tablespoons butter in small saucepan over low heat. Add remaining 1 tablespoon oil, garlic, remaining ½ teaspoon salt and garlic powder; cook over very low heat 5 minutes. Pour into small bowl; set aside.

3 Preheat oven to 400°F. Line baking sheet with parchment paper.

4 Turn out dough onto lightly floured surface; shape into a ball. Let stand 10 minutes. Roll out dough into 8×10-inch rectangle. Cut into 20 squares. Roll each piece into 8-inch rope; tie in a knot. Brush knots with garlic mixture; place on prepared baking sheet.

5 Bake 10 minutes or until knots are lightly browned. Meanwhile, melt remaining 2 tablespoons butter. Combine cheese, parsley and oregano in small bowl; mix well. Brush melted butter over baked knots; immediately sprinkle with cheese mixture. Cool slightly; serve warm.

SUPER SIMPLE CHEESY BUBBLE LOAF

MAKES 12 SERVINGS

- **2 packages (7½ ounces each) refrigerated buttermilk biscuits (10 biscuits per package)**
- **2 tablespoons butter, melted**
- **1½ cups (6 ounces) shredded Italian cheese blend**

1 Preheat oven to 350°F. Spray 9×5-inch loaf pan with nonstick cooking spray.

2 Separate biscuits; cut each biscuit into four pieces with scissors. Layer half of biscuit pieces in prepared pan. Drizzle with 1 tablespoon butter; sprinkle with 1 cup cheese. Top with remaining biscuit pieces, 1 tablespoon butter and ½ cup cheese.

3 Bake about 25 minutes or until golden brown. Serve warm.

TIP: It's easy to change up the flavors in this simple bread. Try Mexican cheese blend instead of Italian, and add taco seasoning and/or hot pepper sauce to the melted butter before drizzling it over the dough. Or, sprinkle ¼ cup chopped ham, salami or crumbled crisp-cooked bacon between the layers of dough.

SOCCA (NIÇOISE CHICKPEA PANCAKE)

MAKES 6 SERVINGS

1 cup chickpea flour

¾ teaspoon salt

½ teaspoon black pepper

1 cup water

5 tablespoons olive oil, divided

1½ teaspoons minced fresh basil *or* ½ teaspoon dried basil

1 teaspoon minced fresh rosemary *or* ¼ teaspoon dried rosemary

¼ teaspoon dried thyme

1 Sift chickpea flour into medium bowl. Stir in salt and pepper. Gradually whisk in water until smooth. Stir in 2 tablespoons oil. Let stand at least 30 minutes.

2 Preheat oven to 450°F. Place 9- or 10-inch cast iron skillet in oven to heat.

3 Add basil, rosemary and thyme to batter; whisk until smooth. Carefully remove skillet from oven. Add 2 tablespoons oil to skillet, swirling to coat pan evenly. Immediately pour in batter.

4 Bake 12 to 15 minutes or until edge of pancake begins to pull away from side of pan and center is firm. Remove from oven. Preheat broiler.

5 Brush with remaining 1 tablespoon oil. Broil 2 to 4 minutes or until dark brown in spots. Cut into wedges. Serve warm.

TIP: Socca are pancakes made of chickpea flour and are commonly served in paper cones as a savory street food in the south of France, especially around Nice.

NOTE: To make a thinner, softer crêpe, just increase the amount of water in the recipe by about ¼ cup and cook in batches in a skillet.

BRAZILIAN CHEESE ROLLS (PÃO DE QUEIJO)

MAKES ABOUT 20 ROLLS

---

1 cup whole milk

¼ cup (½ stick) butter, cut into pieces

¼ cup vegetable oil

2 cups plus 2 tablespoons tapioca flour*

2 eggs

1 cup grated Parmesan cheese or other firm cheese

Sometimes labeled tapioca starch.

1 Preheat oven to 350°F.

2 Combine milk, butter and oil in large saucepan. Heat to a boil over medium heat, stirring to melt butter. Once mixture reaches a boil, remove from heat. Stir in tapioca flour. Mixture will be thick and stretchy.

3 Stir in eggs, one at a time, and cheese. Mixture will be very stiff. Cool mixture in pan until easy to handle.

4 Take heaping tablespoons of dough with tapioca-floured hands and roll into 1½-inch balls. Place on baking sheet about 1 inch apart.

5 Bake 20 to 25 minutes or until puffed and golden. Serve warm.

NOTE: These moist, chewy rolls are a Brazilian specialty and are always made with tapioca flour instead of wheat flour. In Brazil they are popular at breakfast, lunch or dinner.

BEER, CARAMELIZED ONION, BACON AND PARMESAN MUFFINS

MAKES 12 SERVINGS

- **6 slices bacon, chopped**
- **2 cups chopped onions**
- **3 teaspoons sugar, divided**
- **¼ teaspoon dried thyme**
- **1½ cups all-purpose flour**
- **¾ cup grated Parmesan cheese**
- **2 teaspoons baking powder**
- **½ teaspoon salt**
- **¾ cup lager or other light-colored beer**
- **2 eggs**
- **¼ cup extra virgin olive oil**

1 Preheat oven to 375°F. Grease 12 standard (2½-inch) muffin cups.

2 Cook bacon in large skillet over medium heat until crisp, stirring occasionally. Drain on paper towel-lined plate. Add onions, 1 teaspoon sugar and thyme to skillet; cook 12 minutes or until onions are golden brown, stirring occasionally. Cool 5 minutes; stir in bacon.

3 Combine flour, cheese, baking powder, salt and remaining 2 teaspoons sugar in large bowl. Whisk lager, eggs and oil in medium bowl. Add to flour mixture; stir just until dry ingredients are moistened. Gently stir in onion mixture. Spoon batter evenly into prepared muffin cups.

4 Bake 15 minutes or until toothpick inserted into centers comes out clean. Cool in pan 5 minutes; remove to wire rack. Serve warm.

PRETZEL MONKEY BREAD

MAKES 12 SERVINGS

2½ cups all-purpose flour

1½ teaspoons rapid-rise active dry yeast

1 teaspoon sugar

¼ teaspoon salt

¾ cup warm water (120°F)

6 tablespoons butter, melted, divided

½ cup baking soda

Coarse salt

6 tablespoons sour cream

2 tablespoons Dijon mustard

1 tablespoon honey

1 Combine flour, yeast, sugar and ¼ teaspoon salt in large bowl of electric stand mixer. Stir in ¾ cup water and 2 tablespoons melted butter to form rough dough. Knead with dough hook at low speed 5 to 7 minutes or until dough is smooth and elastic. Shape dough into a ball. Place in large lightly greased bowl; turn to grease top. Cover and let rise in warm place about 1 hour or until doubled in size.

2 Preheat oven to 400°F. Line baking sheet with foil; set aside. Brush 9-inch springform pan with 1 tablespoon butter. Spray outside of 6-ounce ramekin with nonstick cooking spray; place in center of pan. Turn out dough onto floured surface; pat and stretch into 12×6-inch rectangle. Cut dough into 1-inch pieces.

3 Bring 12 cups water to a boil in large saucepan; add baking soda. Working in batches, add dough pieces to boiling water; cook 30 seconds. Place half of hot dough pieces around ramekin in prepared pan; brush with half of remaining butter and sprinkle with coarse salt. Top with remaining dough pieces; brush with remaining butter and sprinkle with coarse salt. Place springform pan on prepared baking sheet.

4 Bake about 30 minutes or until pretzels are dark golden brown. Loosen edges of bread with knife; carefully remove side of pan.

5 For dipping sauce, combine sour cream, mustard and honey in small bowl. Carefully remove hot ramekin from center of pretzel ring and replace with bowl of sauce. (Ramekin from oven will be too hot for sauce.) Serve warm.

CHEDDAR BISCUITS

MAKES 15 SERVINGS

- 2 cups all-purpose flour
- 1 tablespoon sugar
- 1 tablespoon baking powder
- 2¼ teaspoons garlic powder, divided
- ¾ teaspoon plus pinch of salt, divided
- 1 cup whole milk
- ½ cup (1 stick) plus 3 tablespoons butter, melted, divided
- 2 cups (8 ounces) shredded Cheddar cheese
- ½ teaspoon dried parsley flakes

1 Preheat oven to 450°F. Line large baking sheet with parchment paper.

2 Combine flour, sugar, baking powder, 2 teaspoons garlic powder and ¾ teaspoon salt in large bowl; mix well. Add milk and ½ cup melted butter; stir just until dry ingredients are moistened. Stir in cheese just until blended. Drop scant ¼ cupfuls of dough about 1½ inches apart onto prepared baking sheet.

3 Bake 10 to 12 minutes or until golden brown. Meanwhile, combine remaining 3 tablespoons melted butter, ¼ teaspoon garlic powder, pinch of salt and parsley flakes in small bowl; brush over biscuits immediately after removing from oven. Serve warm.

SANDWICHES & TOASTS

MOZZARELLA IN CARROZZA
MAKES ABOUT 8 APPETIZER SERVINGS

2 eggs

⅓ cup milk

¼ teaspoon salt

⅛ teaspoon black pepper

8 slices country Italian bread

6 ounces fresh mozzarella, cut into ¼-inch slices

8 oil-packed sun-dried tomatoes, drained and cut into strips

8 to 12 fresh basil leaves, torn

1½ tablespoons olive oil

1 Whisk eggs, milk, salt and pepper in shallow bowl or baking dish until well blended.

2 Place 4 bread slices on work surface. Top with mozzarella, sun-dried tomatoes, basil and remaining bread slices.

3 Heat oil in large skillet over medium heat. Dip sandwiches in egg mixture, turning and pressing to coat completely. Add sandwiches to skillet; cook 5 minutes per side or until golden brown. Cut into strips or squares.

BEANS AND SPINACH BRUSCHETTA

MAKES 16 SERVINGS

---

1 can (about 15 ounces) Great Northern or cannellini beans, rinsed and drained

4 tablespoons extra virgin olive oil, divided

2 cloves garlic, minced

½ teaspoon salt, divided

½ teaspoon black pepper, divided

6 cups loosely packed spinach, finely chopped

1 tablespoon red wine vinegar

16 slices whole grain baguette

1 Purée beans in food processor. (If necessary, add 1 to 2 tablespoons water for smoother texture.) Transfer to medium bowl.

2 Heat 1 tablespoon oil in medium skillet. Add garlic; cook and stir 1 minute. Remove from heat; add ¼ teaspoon salt and ¼ teaspoon pepper. Stir into beans.

3 Heat 1 tablespoon oil in same skillet over medium heat, tilting to coat pan with oil. Add spinach; cook 2 to 3 minutes or until wilted. Stir in vinegar, remaining ¼ teaspoon salt and ¼ teaspoon pepper. Remove from heat.

4 Preheat grill or broiler. Brush baguette slices with remaining 2 tablespoons oil. Grill until bread is golden brown and crisp. Top with bean purée and spinach. Serve immediately.

CHIPOTLE CHICKEN QUESADILLAS

MAKES 20 WEDGES

- **1 package (8 ounces) cream cheese, softened**
- **1 cup (4 ounces) shredded Mexican cheese blend**
- **1 tablespoon minced canned chipotle pepper in adobo sauce**
- **5 (10-inch) flour tortillas**
- **5 cups shredded cooked chicken (about 1¼ pounds)**
- **Guacamole, sour cream, salsa and chopped fresh cilantro**

1 Combine cream cheese, Mexican cheese blend and chipotle pepper in large bowl; mix well.

2 Spread ⅓ cup cheese mixture over half of one tortilla. Top with about 1 cup chicken. Fold tortilla over filling and press gently. Repeat with remaining tortillas, cheese mixture and chicken.

3 Heat large nonstick skillet over medium-high heat. Spray outside surface of each quesadilla with nonstick cooking spray. Cook quesadillas 4 to 6 minutes or until lightly browned, turning once during cooking.

4 Cut each quesadilla into 4 wedges. Serve with guacamole, sour cream, salsa and cilantro.

BLACK BEAN SLIDERS

MAKES 32 MINI SLIDERS

6 tablespoons water

2 tablespoons ground flaxseed (see Note)

1 can (about 15 ounces) black beans, rinsed and drained

2 cloves garlic

¼ teaspoon salt

½ cup chopped onion

½ cup chopped red bell pepper

2 tablespoons chopped fresh parsley

1 cup plain dry bread crumbs

32 mini whole wheat pita bread rounds, cut in half horizontally

Sliced avocado and salsa (optional)

1 Combine water and flaxseed in small saucepan. Bring to a simmer over medium-low heat. Simmer 5 minutes or until thickened. Cool completely.

2 Preheat oven to 375°F. Spray baking sheet with nonstick cooking spray.

3 Combine beans, flaxseed mixture, garlic and salt in food processor or blender; process just until smooth. Add onion, bell pepper and parsley; pulse until combined. Stir in bread crumbs.

4 Shape mixture into 32 (1-inch) patties. Place on prepared baking sheet. Spray patties with cooking spray.

5 Bake 10 minutes. Turn over; bake 10 minutes or until lightly crisped and heated through. Serve in mini pita rounds with avocado and salsa, if desired.

NOTE: This recipe can easily be made non-vegan by substituting 2 eggs for the ground flaxseed and water.

GOAT CHEESE CROSTINI WITH SWEET ONION JAM

MAKES 24 CROSTINI

1 tablespoon olive oil

2 medium yellow onions, thinly sliced

¾ cup dry red wine

¼ cup water

2 tablespoons packed brown sugar

1 tablespoon balsamic vinegar

1 teaspoon salt

¼ teaspoon black pepper

2 ounces soft goat cheese

2 ounces cream cheese, softened

1 teaspoon chopped fresh thyme, plus additional for garnish

1 loaf (16 ounces) French bread, cut into 24 slices (about 1 inch thick), lightly toasted

1 Heat oil in large skillet over medium heat. Add onions; cook and stir 10 minutes. Add wine, water, brown sugar, vinegar, salt and pepper; bring to a simmer. Reduce heat to low; cook 15 to 20 minutes or until all liquid is absorbed. (If mixture appears dry, stir in a few tablespoons of additional water.) Cool 30 minutes or cover and refrigerate until ready to use.

2 Meanwhile, stir goat cheese, cream cheese and 1 teaspoon thyme in small bowl until well blended.

3 Spread ½ teaspoon goat cheese mixture on each slice of bread. Top with 1 teaspoon onion jam. Garnish with additional thyme.

BRUSCHETTA
MAKES 16 CROSTINI (1 CUP TOPPING)

4 plum tomatoes, seeded and diced

½ cup packed fresh basil leaves, finely chopped

5 tablespoons olive oil, divided

2 cloves garlic, minced

2 teaspoons finely chopped oil-packed sun-dried tomatoes

¼ teaspoon salt

⅛ teaspoon black pepper

16 slices Italian bread

2 tablespoons grated Parmesan cheese

1 Combine fresh tomatoes, basil, 3 tablespoons oil, garlic, sun-dried tomatoes, salt and pepper in large bowl; mix well. Let stand at room temperature 1 hour to blend flavors.

2 Preheat oven to 375°F. Place bread on baking sheet. Brush remaining 2 tablespoons oil over one side of each bread slice; sprinkle with cheese. Bake 6 to 8 minutes or until toasted.

3 Top each bread slice with 1 tablespoon tomato mixture.

AVOCADO CROSTINI

MAKES 18 CROSTINI

18 slices French bread, about ¼ inch thick

Olive oil

2 avocados, coarsely chopped

1 clove garlic, minced

2 teaspoons lime juice

Salt and black pepper

2 tablespoons minced red onion

2 tablespoons minced tomato

1 tablespoon minced fresh cilantro

1 Preheat oven to 400°F. Brush bread slices with oil. Place on ungreased baking sheet. Bake 5 minutes or until crisp.

2 Place avocados in small bowl; mash until chunky. Stir in garlic and lime juice; season with salt and pepper. Spread avocado mixture on toasts; top with onion, tomato and cilantro.

CUCUMBER CROSTINI

MAKES 18 CROSTINI

18 slices French bread, about ¼ inch thick

Olive oil

1 cup whipped cream cheese

1 cup finely diced cucumber

2 tablespoons minced fresh dill

Salt and black pepper

Thinly sliced radish and fresh dill sprigs

1 Preheat oven to 400°F. Brush bread slices with oil. Place on ungreased baking sheet. Bake 5 minutes or until crisp.

2 Combine cream cheese, cucumber and minced dill in medium bowl; season with salt and pepper. Spread mixture on toasts; garnish with radish and dill sprigs.

AVOCADO CROSTINI

CUCUMBER CROSTINI

PULLED PORK QUESADILLAS

MAKES 8 SERVINGS

1 **pound pork tenderloin, cut into 3-inch pieces**

1 **cup beer**

1 **cup barbecue sauce**

1 **teaspoon chili powder**

4 **(8-inch) flour tortillas**

2⅔ **cups shredded Monterey jack cheese**

Salsa and sour cream (optional)

1 Combine pork, beer, barbecue sauce and chili powder in large saucepan over medium-high heat; bring to a boil. Reduce heat to medium-low. Cover; simmer 50 minutes or until pork is tender, stirring occasionally. Transfer pork to large bowl; shred using two forks.

2 Bring sauce to a boil over medium-high heat; boil 8 to 10 minutes or until thickened. Add ¾ cup sauce to shredded pork; discard remaining sauce.

3 Place tortillas on work surface. Layer half of each tortilla with pork and cheese. Fold top halves of tortillas over filling to form semicircle.

4 Heat large nonstick skillet over medium heat. Add two quesadillas; cook 6 to 8 minutes or until golden and cheese is melted, turning once. Transfer to cutting board. Cut into six wedges. Repeat with remaining quesadillas.

5 Serve with salsa and sour cream, if desired.

SMOKY BACON MUSHROOM TOASTS

MAKES 24 APPETIZERS

10 slices bacon

1 onion, diced

1 red bell pepper, diced

2 packages (8 ounces each) mushrooms, diced

Salt and black pepper

24 (½-inch) toasted French bread slices

Chopped fresh parsley

1 Cook bacon in large skillet over medium heat until crisp. Drain on paper towels. Discard all but 2 tablespoons drippings from skillet.

2 Add onion and bell pepper to skillet; cook and stir over medium-high heat 2 minutes or until tender. Add mushrooms; season with salt and black pepper. Cook and stir 8 to 10 minutes or until mushroom liquid is almost evaporated. Cool 5 minutes.

3 Crumble bacon. Spread 1½ tablespoons mushroom mixture on each bread slice. Sprinkle with crumbled bacon and parsley.

TOMATO-PESTO CROSTINI

MAKES 16 CROSTINI

1 whole wheat mini baguette (about 4 ounces)

4 plum tomatoes

1 cup (4 ounces) shredded mozzarella cheese

3 tablespoons pesto

1 Preheat oven to 400°F. Slice baguette into 16 very thin diagonal slices. Slice each tomato lengthwise into 4 (¼-inch) slices.

2 Place baguette slices on ungreased baking sheet. Top each with 1 tablespoon cheese and 1 tomato slice.

3 Bake 8 minutes or until bread is lightly toasted and cheese is melted. Top each crostini with about ½ teaspoon pesto. Serve warm.

MINI SWISS STEAK SANDWICHES

MAKES 16 TO 18 SANDWICHES

2 tablespoons all-purpose flour

¼ teaspoon salt

¼ teaspoon black pepper

1¾ pounds boneless beef chuck steak, about 1 inch thick

2 tablespoons vegetable oil

1 onion, sliced

1 green bell pepper, sliced

1 clove garlic, sliced

1 cup canned stewed tomatoes

¾ cup condensed beef consommé, undiluted

2 teaspoons Worcestershire sauce

1 bay leaf

2 tablespoons cornstarch

2 packages (12 ounces each) sweet Hawaiian dinner rolls

SLOW COOKER DIRECTIONS

1 Coat slow cooker with nonstick cooking spray. Combine flour, salt and black pepper in large resealable food storage bag. Add steak; shake to coat.

2 Heat oil in large skillet over high heat. Brown steak on both sides. Transfer to slow cooker.

3 Add onion and bell pepper to skillet; cook and stir over medium-high heat 3 minutes or until softened. Add garlic; cook and stir 30 seconds. Pour mixture over steak.

4 Add tomatoes, consommé, Worcestershire sauce and bay leaf. Cover; cook on HIGH 3½ hours or until steak is tender. Transfer steak to cutting board. Remove and discard bay leaf.

5 Whisk 2 tablespoons cooking liquid into cornstarch in small bowl until smooth. Stir into cooking liquid in slow cooker; cook, uncovered, 10 minutes or until thickened.

6 Thinly slice steak against the grain. Return to slow cooker. Serve steak mixture on rolls.

CHICKPEA, ROASTED PEPPER AND OLIVE TOASTS

MAKES 24 APPETIZERS

2 cloves garlic, peeled

1 can (about 15 ounces) chickpeas, rinsed and drained

1 cup chopped drained roasted red peppers

¼ cup olive oil

Salt and black pepper

½ cup drained pitted black olives

½ cup drained pimiento-stuffed green olives

24 (½-inch) toasted French bread slices

1 Turn on food processor; drop garlic cloves through feed tube. Add chickpeas and roasted peppers; process until paste forms. Add oil; process until smooth. Transfer mixture to medium bowl; season with salt and black pepper. Cover and let stand 30 minutes.

2 Place black and green olives in clean food processor. Process using on/off pulses until olives are coarsely but evenly chopped.

3 Spread 2 tablespoons chickpea mixture on each bread slice. Spoon 1 tablespoon olive mixture in center of chickpea mixture.

NOTE: Leftover chickpea mixture makes a great dip for fresh vegetables.

TIP: Chickpea and olive mixtures can both be prepared up to 2 days in advance. Store separately in airtight containers in the refrigerator.

CROQUE MONSIEUR BITES

MAKES 16 PIECES

8 slices thin firm
sandwich bread

4 slices Swiss cheese,
halved (about
4 ounces)

4 slices smoked ham
(about 4 ounces)

Dash grated nutmeg

2 tablespoons butter,
melted

1 Cut crusts from bread. Place 4 slices on work surface. Layer each with half slice cheese, 1 slice ham and remaining half slice cheese; sprinkle with nutmeg. Top with remaining 4 slices of bread. Brush outsides of sandwiches with melted butter.

2 Cook sandwiches in large skillet over medium heat 2 to 3 minutes per side or until golden brown and cheese is melted. Cut into quarters.

TIP: These sandwiches can be prepared ahead of time and reheated for an easy party appetizer. Leave sandwiches whole after cooking and refrigerate until ready to serve. Cut into quarters and place on foil-lined baking sheet. Bake in preheated 350°F oven 8 minutes or until sandwiches are heated through and cheese is melted.

MINI CHEDDAR-BEER BISCUITS WITH HAM

MAKES 24 BISCUITS

2 cups all-purpose flour

1 tablespoon baking powder

½ teaspoon salt

1 cup (about 4 ounces) shredded Cheddar cheese

¼ cup shortening

¾ cup lager

1 egg, lightly beaten

8 deli ham slices

1 tablespoon honey mustard

1 Preheat oven to 425°F. Grease baking sheet. Combine flour, baking powder and salt in large bowl. Stir in cheese. Cut in shortening with pastry blender or fingers until mixture resembles coarse crumbs. Add lager; stir just until combined.

2 Divide dough in half. Place half of dough on prepared baking sheet; pat into 6×4½-inch rectangle, about ½ inch thick. Score dough into 12 squares. Repeat with remaining dough.

3 Brush top of dough with egg. Bake 17 minutes or until golden brown. Cool on baking sheet 2 minutes. Remove to wire rack; cool completely.

4 Split 1 rectangle horizontally. Arrange 4 slices of ham to cover biscuit bottom. Spread 1½ teaspoons mustard on underside of biscuit top; place on ham. Repeat with remaining ingredients. Cut along score lines into 24 individual biscuits.

ITALIAN SUB CROSTINI

MAKES 12 CROSTINI

1 small loaf (6 inches)
   French bread, cut
   into ½-inch slices

Olive oil

1 ball (8 ounces) fresh
   mozzarella cheese,
   cut into 12 slices

8 ounces sliced
   prosciutto

Fresh basil leaves
   (optional)

1 Preheat oven to 400°F. Brush bread slices with oil. Place on ungreased baking sheet. Bake 5 minutes or until crisp.

2 Place one slice mozzarella on each toast. Top each with one slice of prosciutto.

3 Bake 3 minutes or until cheese is softened. Garnish with basil. Serve immediately.

STUFFED PARTY BAGUETTE

MAKES 12 SERVINGS

2 medium red bell
   peppers

1 loaf French bread
   (about 14 inches
   long)

¼ cup plus
   2 tablespoons Italian
   dressing, divided

1 small red onion, very
   thinly sliced

8 large fresh basil
   leaves

3 ounces Swiss cheese,
   very thinly sliced

1 Preheat oven to 425°F. Cover large baking sheet with foil.

2 To roast bell peppers, cut in half; remove stems, seeds and membranes. Place peppers, cut sides down, on prepared baking sheet. Bake 20 to 25 minutes or until skins are browned.

3 Transfer peppers to paper bag; close bag. Let stand 10 minutes or until peppers are cool enough to handle and skins are loosened. Peel off and discard skins; cut peppers into strips.

4 Trim ends from bread. Cut loaf in half lengthwise. Scoop out soft insides of loaf and reserve for another use.

5 Brush ¼ cup Italian dressing evenly over cut sides of bread. Arrange pepper strips on bottom half of loaf; top with onion. Brush onion with remaining 2 tablespoons Italian dressing; top with basil and cheese. Replace bread top. Wrap loaf tightly in plastic wrap; refrigerate at least 2 hours.

6 To serve, remove plastic wrap. Cut loaf crosswise into 1-inch slices. Secure with toothpicks.

HERBED TUNA SALAD TOASTS

MAKES 24 APPETIZERS

- **3 tablespoons sherry vinegar or red wine vinegar**
- **1 teaspoon coarse grain mustard**
- **¼ cup olive oil**
- **2 cans (6 ounces each) solid white tuna packed in water, drained**
- **2 hard-cooked eggs, peeled and grated**
- **3 green onions, finely chopped**
- **3 tablespoons capers, rinsed and drained**
- **1½ tablespoons chopped fresh oregano**
- **1 tablespoon chopped fresh thyme**
- **2 cloves garlic, minced**
- **Salt and black pepper**
- **24 (½-inch) toasted French bread slices**
- **Smoked paprika or paprika**

1 For vinaigrette, whisk vinegar and mustard in small bowl until blended. Whisk in oil in thin steady stream until well blended.

2 Combine tuna, eggs, green onions, capers, oregano, thyme and garlic in medium bowl; season with salt and pepper. Drizzle vinaigrette over tuna mixture, stirring gently to blend. Refrigerate 2 hours or overnight to allow flavors to blend.

3 Spoon tuna mixture onto bread slices. Sprinkle lightly with paprika. Serve cold or at room temperature.

SNACK MIXES & NUTS

PARMESAN RANCH SNACK MIX

MAKES ABOUT 9½ CUPS

---

3 cups corn or rice cereal squares

2 cups oyster crackers

1 package (5 ounces) bagel chips, broken in half

1½ cups mini pretzel twists

1 cup pistachio nuts

2 tablespoons grated Parmesan cheese

¼ cup (½ stick) butter, melted

1 package (1 ounce) dry ranch salad dressing mix

½ teaspoon garlic powder

SLOW COOKER DIRECTIONS

1 Combine cereal, crackers, bagel chips, pretzels, pistachios and cheese in slow cooker; mix gently.

2 Combine butter, salad dressing mix and garlic powder in small bowl. Pour over cereal mixture; toss lightly to coat. Cover; cook on LOW 3 hours.

3 Stir gently. Cook, uncovered, on LOW 30 minutes.

COCOA-COVERED NUT CLUSTERS

MAKES ABOUT 15 PIECES

2 egg whites, at room temperature

1½ cups walnut halves

1¼ cups pecan halves

¾ cup macadamia nuts, blanched hazelnuts or whole raw almonds

½ cup sugar

6 tablespoons unsweetened cocoa powder

½ teaspoon ground cinnamon

¼ teaspoon salt

1 Preheat oven to 250°F. Line baking sheet with parchment paper.

2 Beat egg whites in large bowl until foamy. Stir in walnuts, pecans, macadamia nuts, sugar, cocoa, cinnamon and salt with wooden spoon until nuts are coated.

3 Spread nut mixture on baking sheet. Bake 30 minutes, stirring every 10 minutes. Cool completely on baking sheet on wire rack. Break into small clusters.

NOTE: Refrigerate leftover nut clusters in a container with a tight-fitting lid.

GARLIC-PARMESAN POPCORN

MAKES 12 CUPS POPCORN

12 cups plain popped
    popcorn

1 tablespoon olive oil

1 tablespoon butter,
    melted

1 clove garlic, finely
    minced

⅓ cup finely grated
    Parmesan cheese

½ teaspoon dried basil

½ teaspoon dried
    oregano

¼ teaspoon salt

1 Place popcorn in large bowl.

2 Combine oil, butter and garlic in small bowl until well blended. Pour over popcorn; toss to coat. Sprinkle with cheese, basil, oregano and salt.

TIP: One regular-size microwavable package of popcorn yields about 10 to 12 cups of popped popcorn.

PEPPY SNACK MIX

MAKES 4 CUPS

3 (3-inch) plain rice cakes, broken into bite-size pieces

1½ cups bite-size frosted shredded wheat cereal

¾ cup pretzel sticks, halved

3 tablespoons butter, melted

2 teaspoons Worcestershire sauce

¾ teaspoon chili powder

⅛ to ¼ teaspoon ground red pepper

1 Preheat oven to 300°F.

2 Combine rice cake pieces, cereal and pretzels in 13×9-inch baking pan. Combine butter, Worcestershire sauce, chili powder and red pepper in small bowl. Drizzle over cereal mixture; toss to combine.

3 Bake 20 minutes, stirring after 10 minutes. Cool completely before serving.

SWEET AND SPICY BEER NUTS

MAKES 3 CUPS

2 cups pecan halves

2 teaspoons salt

2 teaspoons chili powder

2 teaspoons olive oil

½ teaspoon ground cumin

¼ teaspoon ground red pepper

½ cup sugar

½ cup beer

1 Preheat oven to 350°F. Line baking sheet with foil.

2 Mix pecans, salt, chili powder, oil, cumin and red pepper in small bowl. Spread on prepared baking sheet. Bake 10 minutes or until fragrant. Cool on baking sheet on wire rack.

3 Combine sugar and beer in medium saucepan. Cook over medium-high heat until mixture registers 250°F on candy thermometer. Remove from heat; carefully stir in nuts and any loose spices. Spread sugared nuts on baking sheet, separating clusters.

4 Let cool completely. Break up any large pieces before serving.

NUTTY GINGER SNACK MIX

MAKES 2 CUPS

½ cup finely diced crystallized ginger* (about 2½ ounces)

½ cup toasted pine nuts** (about 2½ ounces)

½ cup roasted salted pepitas or pumpkin seeds (about 2 ounces)

½ cup toasted unsalted slivered almonds** (about 2 ounces)

*Spray knife with nonstick cooking spray to prevent sticking.

**To toast nuts, spread in single layer in heavy skillet. Cook over medium heat 1 to 2 minutes or until nuts are lightly browned, stirring frequently. Cool before using.

1 Combine all ingredients in large bowl; mix well.

2 Serve as a snack or use as a topping on vanilla ice cream.

FUDGY MARSHMALLOW POPCORN

MAKES ABOUT 4 QUARTS

3½ **quarts popped popcorn (about 14 cups)**

2 **cups sugar**

1 **cup evaporated milk**

¼ **cup (½ stick) butter**

1 **cup (½ of 7-ounce jar) marshmallow creme**

1 **cup semisweet chocolate chips**

1 **teaspoon vanilla**

1 Spray baking sheets with nonstick cooking spray or line with parchment paper. Place popcorn in large bowl.

2 Combine sugar, evaporated milk and butter in medium saucepan. Cook over medium heat until sugar is dissolved and mixture comes to a boil, stirring constantly. Boil 5 minutes. Remove from heat. Stir in marshmallow creme, chocolate chips and vanilla until chocolate is melted and mixture is smooth.

3 Pour chocolate mixture over popcorn, stirring until completely coated. Spread in single layer on prepared baking sheets. Refrigerate until set.

HINT: Remove any unpopped kernels before measuring the popped popcorn.

CHOCO-PEANUT BUTTER POPCORN

MAKES 4 CUPS

⅓ cup semisweet
  chocolate chips

3 tablespoons natural
  creamy peanut
  butter

1 tablespoon butter

4 cups air-popped
  popcorn

½ cup powdered sugar

1 Microwave chocolate chips, peanut butter
  and butter in medium microwavable bowl
  on HIGH 30 seconds; stir. Microwave
  30 seconds or until melted and smooth.
  Pour mixture over popcorn in large bowl,
  stirring until evenly coated. Transfer to
  1-gallon resealable food storage bag.

2 Add powdered sugar to bag; seal bag and
  shake until well coated. Spread on waxed
  paper to cool.

SOUTHWEST SNACK MIX

MAKES ABOUT 6 CUPS

4 cups corn cereal squares

2 cups pretzel twists

½ cup pumpkin or squash seeds

1½ teaspoons chili powder

1 teaspoon minced fresh cilantro or parsley

½ teaspoon salt

½ teaspoon garlic powder

½ teaspoon onion powder

1 egg white

2 tablespoons olive oil

2 tablespoons lime juice

1 Preheat oven to 300°F. Spray baking sheet with nonstick cooking spray.

2 Combine cereal, pretzels and pumpkin seeds in large bowl. Combine chili powder, cilantro, salt, garlic powder and onion powder in small bowl.

3 Whisk egg white, oil and lime juice in separate small bowl until well blended. Pour over cereal mixture; toss to coat. Add seasoning mixture; mix lightly to coat evenly. Transfer to prepared baking sheet.

4 Bake 45 minutes, stirring every 15 minutes. Cool completely. Store in airtight container.

VARIATION: Substitute ½ cup peanuts for pumpkin seeds.

CITRUS CANDIED NUTS

MAKES ABOUT 3 CUPS

1 egg white

1½ cups whole almonds

1½ cups pecan halves

1 cup powdered sugar

2 tablespoons lemon juice

2 teaspoons grated orange peel

1 teaspoon grated lemon peel

⅛ teaspoon ground nutmeg

1 Preheat oven to 300°F. Grease 15×10-inch baking sheet pan.

2 Beat egg white in medium bowl with electric mixer on high speed until soft peaks form. Add almonds and pecans; stir until well coated. Stir in powdered sugar, lemon juice, orange peel, lemon peel and nutmeg until evenly coated. Spread nuts in single layer in prepared pan.

3 Bake 30 minutes, stirring after 20 minutes. Turn off heat. Let nuts stand in oven 15 minutes. Remove nuts from pan to sheet of foil. Cool completely. Store in airtight container up to 2 weeks.

CINNAMON CARAMEL CORN

MAKES 4 SERVINGS

8 cups air-popped popcorn (about ⅓ cup kernels)

2 tablespoons honey

2 tablespoons butter

¼ teaspoon ground cinnamon

1 Preheat oven to 350°F. Spray jelly-roll pan with nonstick cooking spray. Place popcorn in large bowl.

2 Combine honey, butter and cinnamon in small saucepan; cook and stir over low heat until butter is melted and mixture is smooth. Pour over popcorn; toss to coat evenly. Spread on prepared pan.

3 Bake 12 to 14 minutes or until coating is golden brown and appears crackled, stirring twice.

4 Cool popcorn on pan. (As popcorn cools, coating becomes crisp. If not crisp enough, or if popcorn softens upon standing, return to oven and heat 5 to 8 minutes.) Store in airtight container.

CAJUN POPCORN: Replace cinnamon with 1 teaspoon Cajun or Creole seasoning and add 1 extra teaspoon honey.

SWEET SNACKS

NEW ORLEANS-STYLE PRALINES
MAKES ABOUT 34 PRALINES (1¼ POUNDS)

2 cups packed brown sugar

1 cup half-and-half

½ teaspoon salt

2 tablespoons butter

2 tablespoons bourbon or cognac *or* 1 teaspoon vanilla

1 package (10 ounces) chopped pecans (about 2½ cups), toasted

1 Line two baking sheets with parchment paper or foil. Combine brown sugar, half-and-half and salt in heavy medium saucepan. Cook over medium heat until sugar is dissolved and mixture begins to boil, stirring occasionally.

2 Attach candy thermometer to side of pan, making sure bulb is submerged in sugar mixture but not touching bottom of pan. Continue boiling about 20 minutes or until sugar mixture reaches soft-ball stage (235° to 240°F) on candy thermometer, stirring occasionally. (Watch carefully; candy will be grainy if overcooked.) Remove from heat; stir in butter and bourbon. Stir in pecans.

3 Working quickly, drop mixture by tablespoonfuls onto prepared baking sheets. (If mixture becomes too thick, stir in 1 to 2 teaspoons hot water and reheat over medium heat.) Cool completely, about 30 minutes. Store in airtight container at room temperature up to 3 days.

TINY PEANUT BUTTER SANDWICHES

MAKES 6 TO 7 DOZEN SANDWICHES

1¼ cups all-purpose flour

½ teaspoon baking powder

½ teaspoon baking soda

¼ teaspoon salt

½ cup (1 stick) butter, softened

½ cup granulated sugar

½ cup packed brown sugar

½ cup creamy peanut butter

1 egg

1 teaspoon vanilla

1 cup semisweet chocolate chips

½ cup whipping cream

1 Preheat oven to 350°F. Combine flour, baking powder, baking soda and salt in medium bowl.

2 Beat butter, granulated sugar and brown sugar in large bowl with electric mixer on medium speed until light and fluffy. Beat in peanut butter, egg and vanilla until well blended. Gradually beat in flour mixture on low speed until blended.

3 Shape dough by ½ teaspoonfuls into balls; place 1 inch apart on ungreased cookie sheets. Flatten balls slightly in criss-cross pattern with fork.

4 Bake 6 minutes or just until set. Cool on cookie sheets 4 minutes. Remove to wire racks; cool completely.

5 For filling, place chocolate chips in medium bowl. Place cream in small microwavable bowl; microwave on HIGH 2 minutes or just until simmering; pour over chocolate chips. Let stand 2 minutes; stir until smooth. Let stand 10 minutes or until filling thickens to desired consistency.

6 Spread scant teaspoon filling on flat side of half of cookies; top with remaining cookies. Store in airtight container.

RUSTIC APPLE GALETTES

MAKES 5 TARTLETS

1 tablespoon butter

4 medium Granny Smith, Crispin or other firm-fleshed apples, peeled and cut into ¾-inch chunks (about 4 cups)

6 tablespoons granulated sugar

½ teaspoon ground cinnamon

⅛ teaspoon salt

2 teaspoons cornstarch

2 teaspoons lemon juice

1 refrigerated pie crust (half of 15-ounce package)

1 egg, beaten

1 tablespoon coarse or granulated sugar

1 Melt butter in medium saucepan over medium heat; stir in apples, granulated sugar, cinnamon and salt. Cook 10 minutes or until apples are tender, stirring occasionally. Drain apples in colander set over medium bowl; pour liquid back into saucepan. Cook over medium-high heat until liquid is slightly syrupy and reduced by half. Stir in cornstarch; cook 1 minute.

2 Combine apples, lemon juice and cornstarch mixture in medium bowl; toss to coat. Let cool to room temperature.

3 Preheat oven to 425°F. Line large rimmed baking sheet with parchment paper. Unroll pie crust on work surface; cut out five circles with 4-inch round cookie cutter. Place dough circles on prepared baking sheet.

4 Divide apples evenly among dough circles, piling apples in center of each circle and leaving ½-inch border. Fold edges of dough up over filling, overlapping and pleating dough as necessary. Press dough gently to adhere to filling. Brush dough lightly with beaten egg; sprinkle with coarse sugar.

5 Bake about 25 minutes or until crusts are golden brown. Cool on wire rack.

ONE-BITE CHOCOLATE CHIP COOKIES

MAKES ABOUT 14 DOZEN COOKIES

1¼ cups all-purpose flour

½ teaspoon baking soda

¼ teaspoon salt

½ cup (1 stick) butter, softened

½ cup packed brown sugar

¼ cup granulated sugar

1 egg

1 teaspoon vanilla

1¼ cups mini semisweet chocolate chips

Sea salt (optional)

1 Preheat oven to 350°F. Combine flour, baking soda and salt in medium bowl.

2 Beat butter, brown sugar and granulated sugar in large bowl with electric mixer on medium speed until light and fluffy. Beat in egg and vanilla until blended. Add flour mixture; beat on low speed until well blended. Stir in chocolate chips.

3 Drop dough by ½ teaspoonfuls 1 inch apart onto ungreased cookie sheets. Sprinkle very lightly with sea salt, if desired.

4 Bake 6 minutes or just until edges are golden brown. (Centers of cookies will be very light and will not look done.) Cool on cookie sheets 2 minutes. Remove to wire racks; cool completely.

CLASSIC ENGLISH TOFFEE

MAKES ABOUT 1¼ POUNDS TOFFEE

1 cup (2 sticks) unsalted butter

1 cup sugar

2 tablespoons water

¼ teaspoon salt

1 teaspoon vanilla

3 ounces semisweet chocolate

3 ounces bittersweet chocolate

½ cup chopped toasted pecans*

*To toast pecans, spread in single layer in heavy skillet. Cook and stir over medium heat 1 to 2 minutes or until nuts are lightly browned, stirring frequently.

1 Line 9-inch square pan with heavy-duty foil, leaving 1-inch overhang on all sides.

2 Combine butter, sugar, water and salt in heavy 2- or 2½-quart saucepan. Bring to a boil over medium heat, stirring frequently. Attach candy thermometer to side of pan. Continue boiling about 20 minutes or until sugar mixture reaches hard-crack stage (305° to 310°F), stirring frequently. Watch closely after temperature reaches 290°F. Temperature will rise quickly and mixture will burn above 310°F.) Remove from heat; stir in vanilla. Immediately pour into prepared pan, spreading to edges. Cool completely.

3 Microwave chocolates in small microwavable bowl on MEDIUM (50%) 5 to 6 minutes or until melted, stirring every 2 minutes.

4 Spread chocolate evenly over toffee. Sprinkle chocolate with pecans. Refrigerate about 35 minutes or until chocolate is set.

5 Carefully break toffee into pieces without dislodging pecans. Store in airtight container at room temperature between sheets of waxed paper.

SALTED CARAMEL POPS

MAKES 12 POPS

1 pint (2 cups) vanilla
   ice cream

1 cup finely chopped
   salted pretzel sticks
   (about 2 cups whole
   pretzels)

¼ cup caramel ice cream
   topping

Coarse salt

Pop sticks

2 ounces semisweet
   chocolate

1 Scoop ice cream into chilled large metal
   bowl. Cut in pretzels and caramel topping
   with pastry blender or two knives; fold and
   cut again. Repeat, working quickly, until
   mixture is evenly incorporated. Cover and
   freeze 1 hour.

2 Line small baking sheet with plastic wrap.
   Scoop 12 balls of ice cream mixture onto
   prepared baking sheet. Freeze 1 hour.

3 Shape ice cream into balls, if necessary.
   Evenly sprinkle ice cream balls with salt.
   Insert sticks. Freeze 1 hour or until firm.

4 Melt chocolate in top of double boiler over
   simmering water, stirring occasionally.

5 Drizzle melted chocolate over pops. Freeze
   30 minutes to 1 hour or until firm.

BUTTERSCOTCH-CHOCOLATE DIVINITY

MAKES ABOUT 36 PIECES

2 cups sugar

⅓ cup light corn syrup

⅓ cup water

2 egg whites

⅛ teaspoon cream of tartar

1 teaspoon vanilla

½ cup milk chocolate chips

½ cup butterscotch chips

½ cup chopped nuts

1 Line two baking sheets with parchment paper.

2 Combine sugar, corn syrup and water in medium heavy saucepan. Cook over medium heat without stirring until sugar dissolves and mixture comes to a boil. Clip candy thermometer to side of pan, making sure bulb is submerged in sugar mixture but not touching bottom of pan. Continue to cook until mixture reaches the hard-ball stage (255°F).

3 Meanwhile, beat egg whites and cream of tartar in large bowl with electric mixer on high speed until stiff but not dry. With mixer running on high speed, slowly pour hot syrup into egg whites in thin steady stream. Add vanilla; beat until candy forms soft peaks and starts to lose its gloss. Stir in both kinds of chips and nuts with spatula.

4 Working quickly, drop mixture by tablespoonfuls with spoon or small cookie scoop onto prepared baking sheets. Store in refrigerator in airtight container between layers of waxed paper or freeze up to 3 months.

CHOCOLATE PEANUT CRUNCH

MAKES ABOUT ¾ POUND

1 cup milk chocolate chips

½ cup semisweet chocolate chips

2 tablespoons corn syrup

1 tablespoon shortening

½ cup unsalted roasted peanuts

2 teaspoons vanilla

1 Butter 8-inch square baking pan.

2 Melt milk and semisweet chocolate chips with corn syrup and shortening in small heavy saucepan over low heat, stirring constantly.

3 Stir in peanuts and vanilla. Spread in prepared pan, distributing peanuts evenly. Refrigerate until firm. Break into pieces.

GINGER MOLASSES SPICE COOKIES

MAKES ABOUT 12 DOZEN COOKIES

2 cups all-purpose flour

1½ teaspoons ground ginger

1 teaspoon baking soda

½ teaspoon salt

½ teaspoon ground cinnamon

½ teaspoon ground cloves

1¼ cups sugar, divided

¾ cup (1½ sticks) butter, softened

¼ cup molasses

1 egg

1 Preheat oven to 375°F. Combine flour, ginger, baking soda, salt, cinnamon and cloves in medium bowl.

2 Beat 1 cup sugar and butter in large bowl with electric mixer on medium speed until light and fluffy. Add molasses and egg; beat until well blended. Gradually beat in flour mixture on low speed just until blended.

3 Place remaining ¼ cup sugar in shallow bowl. Shape dough by ½ teaspoonfuls into balls; roll in sugar to coat. Place 1 inch apart on ungreased cookie sheets.

4 Bake 7 to 8 minutes or until almost set. Cool on cookie sheets 2 minutes. Remove to wire racks; cool completely.

CHOCOLATE-COVERED BACON

MAKES 12 SLICES

12 slices thick-cut bacon

12 wooden skewers
(12 inches)

1 cup semisweet
chocolate chips

2 tablespoons
shortening, divided

1 cup white
chocolate chips or
butterscotch chips

1 Preheat oven to 400°F. Thread each bacon slice onto wooden skewer. Place on rack in large baking pan. Bake 20 to 25 minutes or until crisp. Cool completely.

2 Combine semisweet chocolate chips and 1 tablespoon shortening in large microwavable bowl. Microwave on HIGH at 30-second intervals until melted and smooth.

3 Combine white chocolate chips and remaining 1 tablespoon shortening in large microwavable bowl. Microwave on HIGH at 30-second intervals until melted and smooth.

4 Drizzle chocolates over each bacon slice as desired. Place on waxed paper-lined baking sheets. Refrigerate until firm. Store in refrigerator.

INDEX

METRIC CONVERSION CHART

VOLUME MEASUREMENTS (dry)

1/8 teaspoon = 0.5 mL
1/4 teaspoon = 1 mL
1/2 teaspoon = 2 mL
3/4 teaspoon = 4 mL
1 teaspoon = 5 mL
1 tablespoon = 15 mL
2 tablespoons = 30 mL
1/4 cup = 60 mL
1/3 cup = 75 mL
1/2 cup = 125 mL
2/3 cup = 150 mL
3/4 cup = 175 mL
1 cup = 250 mL
2 cups = 1 pint = 500 mL
3 cups = 750 mL
4 cups = 1 quart = 1 L

VOLUME MEASUREMENTS (fluid)

1 fluid ounce (2 tablespoons) = 30 mL
4 fluid ounces (1/2 cup) = 125 mL
8 fluid ounces (1 cup) = 250 mL
12 fluid ounces (1 1/2 cups) = 375 mL
16 fluid ounces (2 cups) = 500 mL

WEIGHTS (mass)

1/2 ounce = 15 g
1 ounce = 30 g
3 ounces = 90 g
4 ounces = 120 g
8 ounces = 225 g
10 ounces = 285 g
12 ounces = 360 g
16 ounces = 1 pound = 450 g

DIMENSIONS

1/16 inch = 2 mm
1/8 inch = 3 mm
1/4 inch = 6 mm
1/2 inch = 1.5 cm
3/4 inch = 2 cm
1 inch = 2.5 cm

OVEN TEMPERATURES

250°F = 120°C
275°F = 140°C
300°F = 150°C
325°F = 160°C
350°F = 180°C
375°F = 190°C
400°F = 200°C
425°F = 220°C
450°F = 230°C

BAKING PAN SIZES

Utensil	Size in Inches/Quarts	Metric Volume	Size in Centimeters
Baking or Cake Pan (square or rectangular)	8×8×2	2 L	20×20×5
	9×9×2	2.5 L	23×23×5
	12×8×2	3 L	30×20×5
	13×9×2	3.5 L	33×23×5
Loaf Pan	8×4×3	1.5 L	20×10×7
	9×5×3	2 L	23×13×7
Round Layer Cake Pan	8×1½	1.2 L	20×4
	9×1½	1.5 L	23×4
Pie Plate	8×1¼	750 mL	20×3
	9×1¼	1 L	23×3
Baking Dish or Casserole	1 quart	1 L	—
	1½ quart	1.5 L	—
	2 quart	2 L	—